James Madison Cutts, Making of America Project, Stephen Arnold Douglas

A Brief Treatise Upon Constitutional and Party Questions

James Madison Cutts,　Making of America Project, Stephen Arnold Douglas

A Brief Treatise Upon Constitutional and Party Questions

ISBN/EAN: 9783744673624

Printed in Europe, USA, Canada, Australia, Japan

Cover: Foto ©ninafisch / pixelio.de

More available books at **www.hansebooks.com**

A BRIEF TREATISE

UPON

CONSTITUTIONAL

AND

PARTY QUESTIONS,

AND

THE HISTORY OF POLITICAL PARTIES,

AS I RECEIVED IT ORALLY FROM THE LATE SENATOR STEPHEN A. DOUGLAS, OF ILLINOIS.

BY

J. MADISON CUTTS,

BREVET LIEUTENANT COLONEL, U. S. A.

NEW YORK:
D. APPLETON AND COMPANY,
443 & 445 BROADWAY.
1866.

Entered, according to Act of Congress, in the year 1866, by
D. APPLETON & CO.,
In the Clerk's Office of the District Court of the United States for the Southern District of New York.

TO THE FRIENDS

OF THE

Hon. STEPHEN A. DOUGLAS,

NORTH, WEST, AND SOUTH;

AND IN AN ESPECIAL MANNER MOST WARMLY AND AFFECTIONATELY

TO THE

Hon. DANIEL P. RHODES,

OF CLEVELAND, OHIO,

HIS RELATIVE, VERY DEAR FRIEND, AND FAITHFUL EXECUTOR,

THIS VOLUME

IS RESPECTFULLY DEDICATED.

PREFACE.

In the summer of 1859 Mr. Douglas remained in Washington; and as I was very desirous of receiving from him a statement of his own political faith, with the general views of a statesman upon Constitutional, Political, and Party Questions, I prepared, with his consent, a brief analysis of such subjects as I wished him to explain to me. We were in the habit of spending an hour together each evening, until all the questions I had proposed were answered.

The following brief treatise embodies all of these conversations, which were taken down in writing, verbally, at the time—Mr. Douglas always pausing long enough to enable me to obtain his exact language.

As these conversations were not intended for publication, and were entirely free and unrestrained, wanting all of that method and careful thought which the term "treatise" implies,. I have been induced to rely entirely upon the dignity of the subjects discussed, and their general interest to the friends of the late Senator Douglas, to justify the title I have adopted.

I am persuaded that this volume contains a more complete and perfect statement of his opinions than any original work of compilation by another could possibly embody, and that it will be generally acceptable to his friends, and be found worthy of their perusal, *because it came from himself*.

J. MADISON CUTTS,
Brevet Lieutenant Colonel, U. S. A.

NEW YORK CITY, *June* 1, 1866.

CONTENTS.

	PAGE
THE PREAMBLE OF THE CONSTITUTION DISCUSSED,	11
THE LEGISLATIVE POWER OF THE GOVERNMENT,	12
Right of Suffrage under the Constitution,	13
THE POWERS OF CONGRESS CONSIDERED,	16
HISTORY OF THE NATIONAL BANK,	20
Removal of the deposits,	23
Specie circulars,	26
The Sub-Treasury,	27
Popular argument against the Sub-Treasury,	29
Arguments in its favor,	30
The financial policy of the Democratic party adopted by the people,	32
PROHIBITION OF THE AFRICAN SLAVE TRADE,	33
SUSPENSION OF THE WRIT OF HABEAS CORPUS,	35
History of General Jackson's suspension of the writ in New Orleans, and arguments for and against the bill refunding the fine imposed upon him,	37
INTERNAL IMPROVEMENTS, AND RIVER AND HARBOR IMPROVEMENTS,	41
OF THE EXECUTIVE POWER,	47
Power of the President to make removals, and to fill vacancies,	48
OF THE JUDICIAL POWER,	49

	PAGE
SLAVERY,	50
POWER TO ACQUIRE TERRITORY,	51
ADMISSION OF NEW STATES,	52
POWER TO DISPOSE OF PUBLIC PROPERTY,	53
HISTORY OF THE ACQUISITIONS OF TERRITORY BY THE UNITED STATES,	55
1. Of the Louisiana purchase,	55
2. Of Florida, and parts of Alabama, Mississippi, and Louisiana,	59
3. Of Oregon, Texas, California, and New Mexico,	60
The Re-annexation of Texas, Re-occupation of Oregon, and the Mexican war,	61
HISTORY OF THE MISSOURI COMPROMISE,	69
THE WILMOT PROVISO, AND THE COMPROMISE OF 1850,	75
THE KANSAS-NEBRASKA BILL, AND THE SUBSEQUENT HISTORY OF KANSAS UNDER THAT LAW—THE KANSAS-LECOMPTON CONTROVERSY, AND THE PERFIDY OF MR. BUCHANAN AND HIS ADMINISTRATION,	84
POPULAR AND SQUATTER SOVEREIGNTY DEFINED AND DISTINGUISHED,	123
ORIGIN, HISTORY, AND STATE OF PARTIES, FROM THE FORMATION OF THE GOVERNMENT DOWN TO THE ADMINISTRATION OF PRESIDENT PIERCE,	125
Republican and Federal parties,	127
Alien and Sedition Laws,	128
Resolutions of 1798 and 1799,	129
Hartford Convention—War of 1812,	132
The Era of Good Feeling,	133
Defeat of General Jackson,	135
Charges of bribery and corruption against Henry Clay,	137
Democratic party assumes its name,	137
South Carolina Nullification doctrine,	138
General Jackson suppresses nullification,	139

	PAGE
Clay's Compromise Tariff Bill, ...	140
Origin of the name of the Whig party, and its chief measures stated, ...	141
General Jackson reorganizes his Cabinet, ...	148
Mr. Van Buren's rejection by the Senate as minister to England, and his subsequent election as President of the United States, ...	143
Van Buren's Administration, ...	145
Election of General Harrison, his death, Tyler's succession and administration, ...	147
The Texas question: it defeats Mr. Van Buren and Mr. Clay, and elects President Polk, ...	149
Election of General Taylor in consequence of the division in the New York Democracy: this division explained,	155
THE TARIFF—POSITION OF PARTIES THEREON, ...	158
THE PUBLIC LAND SYSTEM OF THE UNITED STATES,	161
THE HOMESTEAD BILL, ...	174
HISTORY OF THE ILLINOIS CENTRAL RAILROAD BILL,	187
INDIANS AND INDIAN INTERCOURSE LAWS, . .	200
THE RECIPROCITY TREATY, ...	203
THE MONROE DOCTRINE, ...	207
CENTRAL AMERICA AND THE CLAYTON-BULWER TREATY, ...	209
THE PACIFIC RAILROAD, ... - . .	217

1*

A BRIEF TREATISE

ON

CONSTITUTIONAL AND PARTY QUESTIONS.

PREAMBLE.

"WE, the people of the United States, in order to form a more perfect Union, establish Justice, insure domestic Tranquillity, provide for the common Defence, promote the general Welfare, and secure the blessings of Liberty to ourselves and our Posterity, do ordain and establish this Constitution for the United States of America."

The Constitution is an amendment, in the form of a substitute, for the Articles of Confederation; the successor of the government of the Confederation. Chief Justice Taney, in the Dred Scott case, says *not :* that it was a *new* government.

"In order to form a *more perfect Union,*" denotes and implies that *it is a continuation.*

"We, the people of the United States."

The Constitution was made by the States, and not by the people united. It should therefore read, "We, the people of the States united." It was voted for by States in the Convention, submitted to the people of each State severally, and became the Constitution *only of the States adopting it.* It is a Federal Constitution, and not a National Government.

"Promote the general Welfare."

The Federalist party contended that this gave Congress power to do whatever it thought would promote the general welfare. But the preamble gives no power. It neither confers, enlarges, nor restrains power; but simply declares the objects for which, and the reasons why the powers *subsequently* and *elsewhere* conferred, were conferred.

ARTICLE FIRST.

OF THE LEGISLATIVE POWER.

In the Confederation all powers were granted to one body, namely, "the United States in Congress assembled." Experience under the Confederation taught that the British system of three departments, with which they had been familiar, was the best. The Constitution was not made, manufactured. It grew as a plant, and was the development of the experience of ages. The Articles of Confederation were a departure from, and they returned to the system with which they had been familiar, both in the British Constitution and in the organization of their own colonial assemblies.

Section 2. " And the electors in each State shall have the qualifications requisite for electors of the most numerous branch of the State Legislature."

One of the great difficulties encountered and overcome in the formation of the Constitution was to determine the Right of Suffrage. Who should be the constituency of the House of Representatives? Should it be uniform in all the States, or not?

Each State had its own system, and wanted it adopted. Some required property qualifications, others not. The compromise was—to let each State adopt its own system, with the limitation contained in the section under consideration. Here I call your attention to two general propositions: 1st. A man may be a citizen and not a voter, and he may be a voter and not a citizen. 2d. Citizen of a State, means citizen of the United States resident in a State.

No power except that of the Federal Government can create a citizen. But the *privileges* may be conferred, by virtue of the *sovereignty* of the State, and are good within its limits.

It is difficult to give a construction, and the courts have only glanced at it. See the Dred Scott decision, where the court decides Dred not a citizen so as to have the right to sue under Art. 3, Sec. 2 of the Constitution.

How many members a State may send, and what their qualifications, is elsewhere determined. But each State is left to decide for itself *who shall send them.* So also as to who shall be the electors of the President. Each State prescribes who shall be, and the manner of the election. May be a negro, a woman, an unnaturalized person, and may be elected in any way. In South Carolina, now, by the Legislature, and formerly so in nearly if not all the States.

The impression is that an unnaturalized person cannot vote for a Federal officer, and so would answer ninety-nine out of a hundred. Design and necessity gave rise to the clause under discussion. I first raised that question. It is reported in Illinois in 1838 or 1839. So that right to vote is not affected by naturalization, and is not one of the rights conferred by naturalization. See the contested case of Jones and Botts of Virginia in 1843. In 1836 the Whigs, Clay among them, opposed the admission of Michigan because she gave unnaturalized persons the right to vote.

Each State may prescribe its own *terms of suffrage*, but cannot prescribe the *qualifications* of the man who is to hold the office. That he should be "an inhabitant of the State in which he shall be chosen," was a provision of the Constitution intended to correct abuses which had sprung up in England.

A State may elect by district, or by general ticket, unless Congress should itself divide the States into districts, but it cannot compel the States to district themselves. See a report made by me upon this subject.

A State cannot so far make a man a citizen as to confer upon him a right to sue in the United States courts. It can only confer upon him such *privileges of citizenship* as its own citizens enjoy, but cannot make him a citizen.

A State cannot enlarge or diminish the qualifications of Senators or Representatives. The only inquiry is, have they the qualifications required by the Constitution, namely, age and inhabitancy of the State in which or for which they are elected. See the case of Trumbull of Illinois, in the Senate, and, at the same time, of Marshall of Illinois, in the House. As to who are "inhabitants," see the cases of Felix Grundy of Tennessee, John Forsyth of Georgia, and Bayly of Massachusetts.

Dallas passed the revenue tariff of 1846 by his casting vote as President of the Senate.

Under Art. I., Sec. 6, Clause 2, a question has arisen, and some have held that the position of minister to a foreign country is not an office under the Constitution, and that the President could appoint one without a law creating. I hold no such thing.

ARTICLE I., SECTION 8.—THE POWERS OF CONGRESS.

You may *strain* a power beyond the *moral right*.

The general rule is, that few of these powers are concurrent, and most of them exclusive. The peculiar phraseology and subject matter give rise to the exceptions in which they are held concurrent.

Art. I., *Sec.* 8, *Clause* 7. The Congress shall have power "to establish Post-Offices and Post-Roads."

But not to construct and build—simply to indicate the line, the route.

"To constitute tribunals inferior to the Supreme Court."

But not to confer a jurisdiction not authorized in the third article of the Constitution.

"To promote the progress of science and the useful arts," etc.

But no power to establish a University. The power is limited to the mode mentioned, namely, "by securing for limited times to authors and inventors the exclusive right to their respective writings and discoveries."

Mr. Madison offered in the Convention a provision which would have authorized the establishment of a University, but it was not adopted.

It has been said that Congress would have power to establish a University in the District of Columbia, on the ground of its exclusive jurisdiction. But exclusive jurisdiction means here, *that there shall be no other*, not that it shall be *unlimited*. *It must be subordinate to the limitations of the Constitution*, and thus confined in its means. It has power to establish schools for the District, but this would not authorize a University in its character national, but might of a local character.

Congress makes appropriations for railroads, for example, the Illinois Central, under its "power to dispose of and make all needful rules and regulations respecting the territory or other property of the United States," conferred in Art. 4, Sec. 3, Clause 2 of the Constitution. It might give the land away, but there is a moral obligation not to do so. Congress gave the land to the Illinois Central, on the ground of the increase of value. The lands had been for forty years unsold. They gave alternate sections, and sold readily the other half for more than they had asked for the whole. There was also a provision that the railroad should carry the mails for a just and fair compensation, which, in case of disagreement, was to be fixed by the Congress. The grant was made to the State, and thence to the company.

Art. I., *Section* 8, *Clause* 18. "To make all laws which shall be necessary and proper for carrying into execution the foregoing powers, and all other powers vested by this Constitution in the Government of the United States, or in any Department or Officer thereof."

This clause confers no new powers. It is only declaratory of a rule of construction, which would have been precisely the same without it; for powers were already given, and necessarily include the means of using them. It would have been implied without this declaration.

"Necessary and proper." Some say essentially, absolutely necessary. But see the reasoning of Chief Justice Marshall in the case of McCulloch *vs.* State of Maryland. Carried to the extent of *his* doctrine, you would substitute the *discretion* of Congress for the Constitution.

The true doctrine is, that where there are several means adapted to the same end, Congress may *fairly choose.* The means must be appropriate and adapted to the end authorized by the Constitution, and that end must be *the one* for which the means *is used*, and not *incidentally* the end proposed. Hence we exclude a National Bank, because you establish it to *issue money*, regulate the currency, while the Treasury Agency *you make incidental.* I will here give you the history of the National Bank.

HISTORY OF THE NATIONAL BANK.

IMMEDIATELY after the first Congress of 1791, Alexander Hamilton, Secretary of the Treasury, recommended a bank, as one of the means necessary to restore the credit of the Government, and to act as its financial agent. The two Houses of Congress, on his recommendation, passed the first bank charter.

General Washington expressed serious doubts of the power to pass the law, and took the opinions of his Cabinet, in writing. Thomas Jefferson, Secretary of State, was against it. Edmund Randolph, Attorney-General, expressed the same opinion; while General Henry Knox, Secretary of War, sustained Hamilton in its constitutionality. Washington referred the opinions of Jefferson and others to Hamilton for his reply, who gave an elaborate opinion, sustaining the right of Congress to establish the bank.

On consideration of the whole subject, General

Washington was of the opinion that the bank was unconstitutional, and that he ought to veto it, and called on Mr. Madison to prepare for him a veto message, which he accordingly did. Upon the presentation of that message, Washington again expressed himself in doubt, inclining to the impression that the power did not exist. Jefferson still adhered to his opinion that it was clearly unconstitutional, but he advised the President, *that in cases of great and serious doubt, the doubt should be weighed in favor of legislative authority. Whereupon Washington signed the bill.*

That first charter ran twenty years, from 1791 to 1811. On application for its renewal in 1811, the Democratic party generally resisted on Constitutional grounds, and the Federal party sustained it. Henry Clay made his first great speech against it in 1811, and the bill for re-charter was defeated, and the bank expired. The war of 1812 immediately intervened. The finance, currency, and credit of the country became greatly disturbed, and an impression was made on the minds of the American people that a bank was necessary to restore them. In 1815 a bank charter passed, received votes from both parties, and opposition from both, and Mr. Madison vetoed it. The next year John C. Calhoun, as a leader in the Republican or Democratic party, introduced a bill, with the sanction of a large portion of the party, for a National Bank. It passed both houses, and Mr. Madison, waiving his scruples, and yielding to what seemed the public opinion of the country, signed it. That charter also ran for twenty years, until 1836, and for the ensuing five years ceased to be a party question. All acquiesced in it, though a great portion of all the leading Democrats still retained their opposition; but it did not go into the elections, and nobody knew whether it would ever become a party question again.

But General Jackson became President in 1829, and, in his message of 1830 or 1831, called the attention of the country to the bank, whose charter would expire in 1836, with intimations of doubts as to its constitutionality. In 1832, preceding the Presidential election, and with a view to influence it, the opponents of General Jackson brought in a bill for the re-charter of the bank, and pressed it through both houses of Congress, in order to compel Jackson to sign it before the election, or to encounter the opposition of the bank, and all its friends, in the coming election. Large numbers of Jackson's best friends, probably including a majority of the leading men in both houses of Congress, urged him to sign the bill. Not that they believed, or pretended to believe, that the bank ought to be re-chartered, but they were clearly of the opinion that if he did veto it, he would be defeated for re-election, and the opposite party would come into power, and not only re-charter the bank, but carry out all their other measures, to which the Democratic party were opposed. Jackson replied, that the bank was *unconstitutional, corrupt,* and *insolvent.* He persisted in declaring it insolvent, though then at 130, but ultimately, not a cent on the dollar. He declared that he would veto it, if it was the last act of his life, and it sank the party with him; telling those of his friends who were afraid of the consequences, that they could desert and go over to the bank, and he would whip the whole of them. He vetoed it on the 10th of July, 1832, and was re-elected by a large majority in November of the same year *on that issue.*

In September, 1833, Duane was removed from the Treasury Department because he refused to remove the deposits, which Jackson insisted on, upon the ground that the bank was corrupt and insolvent, using its funds to control elections, and to corrupt the people. Jackson sent for Roger B. Taney, and said to him, "You are Secretary of the Treasury.

I want the deposits removed." Taney removed them, and then the excitement was still greater. Immediately the bank curtailed discounts in every part of the country at once, and refusing to discount for those who opposed the bank, broke every man not in its favor, still extending loans to those in favor, to buy the property of those who were obliged to sacrifice. The distress was terrible; you can examine for yourself the petitions portraying it. There was the greatest panic, and the wildest frenzy, when Congress met in the winter of 1833.

The Senate passed resolutions of censure. Jackson protested; said he was not before them for impeachment. Many of Jackson's friends deserted him in the House, and they passed resolutions in favor of the return of the deposits. The Government had seven, out of the thirty-five directors of the bank, and Jackson called on them to furnish a list of loans, by which he showed that nearly every member who had deserted him, had received loans from the bank. Henry Clay had got round for the bank, so also had Webster, who, in 1815, was against it, but was now a leader, and for it. It was a Whig measure. But Calhoun, who was the author of the bank charter in 1817, had got round, and *was now declaring it palpably unconstitutional,* but still declared that Jackson had violated the Constitution in removing the deposits, and the opposition to Jackson on that question was conducted by Clay, Calhoun, and Webster, in concert.

Jackson appealed to the people at the next State elections on these questions, on the ground that the bank was unconstitutional and corrupt, using money to control elections and the people, and to buy up their representatives. This was in 1834 and 1835. The people responded, and returned a majority in favor of Jackson and his policy; and the Senate, there being a majority in both Houses in his favor, expunged the resolutions against him.

The bank then again enlarged its discounts, stimulated the prices of property, of stocks, and the importation of goods, and the consequent means of revenue, beyond any parallel known in the world. The revenue was being piled up in the State banks to an unparalleled extent. The banks, on the strength of the surplus not used, increased discounts, which increased importations and revenue. Speculations in the public lands raged in the same ratio, until their sales ran up in 1836 to twenty-four millions, as against the ordinary amount of three millions—all paid for in bank notes, which same went into the bank again, and formed the basis of additional discounts, thus aggravating the evil, until Jackson discovered that unless that system could be checked, the State banks and all the banks in the country would necessarily be exploded, and the whole become insolvent; the Government thus having its revenues piled up in them, which would exist *on their books, but not in fact.* With a view to check this, Jackson issued a circular, called Specie Circular, authorizing all receivers of public money to refuse any thing but gold or silver in payment of duties, or for lands. Instantly speculation was checked, but every speculator became and was the inveterate enemy of Jackson and of his party.

On the 4th of March, 1837, the charter of the National Bank expired, but the State of Pennsylvania had, in the mean time, re-chartered it as a State bank, and under its new organization it had still increased its discounts. In May, 1837, the explosion came. The United States banks and State banks throughout the whole country suspended, beginning in New York and Pennsylvania, and following in every city and town, as the news reached them, until in ten days there was not a specie-paying bank in the country. The Federal Government was instantly reduced to insolvency, without a dollar; the State banks being unable to pay, and the national banks holding on to the specie. Every State became insolvent for the same reason, namely, keeping deposits in the banks, and the banks all failed. Merchants, insurance companies, all failed, and there was universal bankruptcy, Federal, State, and individual, throughout the length and breadth of the land.

Mr. Van Buren being President (1837) immediately issued a proclamation to assemble Congress to provide a revenue, and in his message recommended to Congress his celebrated Sub-Treasury scheme, which in the language of the day, proposed to divorce the Government from all banking institutions, and in place of them, as fiscal agents, to appoint Assistant Treasurers of the United States in the principal cities, who should receive and disburse the public revenue, keeping it in the United States Treasury, and making it a criminal offence to receive or pay any thing but gold or silver, loan any public money, deposit it in any bank, or use it for any but public purposes.

Calhoun joined Van Buren, and dissolved his connection with Clay and Webster on the Sub-Treasury, and the Sub-Treasury then became the issue between the Whigs and Democrats. The banks and speculators all joined the Whigs. The

Sub-Treasury bill passed in 1838 or 1839, and thus freed the Government from the banks.

It took the country many years to recover from the general bankruptcy, and in 1840 the Whigs, with Harrison and Tyler, appealed to the public to make a change in the Government, charging the Democratic party as responsible for all the evils which had befallen the country; that its policy had broken the National Bank and the State banks, and all the moneyed institutions of the country, and brought universal bankruptcy to every man's door, and crushed the merchants. The whole people being convinced that no change could be for the worse, financially speaking, determined to see if it could be for the better. Mr. Van Buren was defeated, carrying but seven States—two free, New Hampshire and Illinois, with five Southern, Virginia, South Carolina, Alabama, Missouri, and Arkansas.

The Whig party having thus acquired the power, proceeded to repeal the Sub-Treasury, and to charter a Bank of the United States, to take its place as the fiscal agent of the Government. General Harrison having died, Mr. Tyler became President, and vetoed the bank charter, in accordance with the principles which he had proclaimed during his whole life. It is here to be remembered that Harrison and Tyler had been elected by the Whigs, but the Whigs during the election had sunk the bank issue, keeping up their opposition to the Sub-Treasury as an issue, and this in order to get the votes of the anti-bank Jackson men, who were opposed to Mr. Van Buren and to his Sub-Treasury policy. But they revived the bank issue the moment they had succeeded in getting power. Harrison and Tyler were both against the bank. Mr. Tyler was always an anti-bank man, but was opposed to the Sub-Treasury. He therefore vetoed the bank charter, but signed the bill repealing the Sub-Treasury.

The popular argument against the Sub-Treasury was, that it provided one currency for the people and another for the Government; that it increased the patronage of the Federal Government, by the appointment of sub-treasurers and agents at great cost, to keep the money, which had been previously kept by the banks for nothing; that it would have the effect of drawing all the gold and silver through land offices and the customs into the Federal Treasury, there to be locked up beyond the reach of the people, thus depriving the banks which furnished the currency of the country from having any specie basis with which to redeem their paper; that it made an odious, unjust distinction between the employés of the Federal Government, who received their pay in specie, and the workingmen throughout the country, who received their wages in broken-bank paper.

The argument in favor was, that by requiring all public dues to be paid in gold and silver, it created a demand for specie, thus increased the specie basis in our currency, and kept the gold *in* the country by its constant circulation in being paid in and out of the Treasury in all Federal operations, in full accordance with the Constitution, which prohibits any other legal tender than gold and silver; that while the old system of depositing the public money in banks stimulated speculation and overtrading by becoming a basis for increased bank issues, which stimulated additional importations, and thus increased the surplus revenue in the banks as the basis again for additional circulation, this process constantly increasing and aggravating the evils which had lead to the explosion, on the other hand requiring gold and silver in payment of revenue, and keeping that revenue in the Treasury of the country, produced a check upon the over-issues of the banks, and tended to restrain the excesses of speculation and overtrading, by withdrawing the surplus revenue from the circulation of the country, and confining the business of the country within its legitimate limits, while at the same time it rendered the Government independent of the banks, by always placing and having its revenue within its own keeping, not exposed to the danger of bank failures.

In addition to the repeal of the Sub-Treasury, and the chartering of a National Bank, the Whigs in 1842 passed a high protective tariff, carrying the protective principle to a greater extent than had ever been done in the history of the country, and at the same time they withdrew their support from Mr. Tyler and his administration, denouncing him and his supporters as traitors to the Whig party for having vetoed the bank, although he had signed their bills for the repeal of the Sub-Treasury and for the protective tariff. Upon the expiration of Mr. Tyler's term of office the Democratic party again regained possession of the Government *on those distinct issues* by the election of Mr. Polk over Mr. Clay. It is proper to remark, however, that during the last years of Mr. Tyler's administration a treaty was made with the Republic of Texas for the annexation of that State to the Federal Union, which having been rejected by the Senate became one of the issues of the Presidential election, supported by the Democrats and opposed by the Whigs. It had not been in the Senate, however, a party question. The *old fogies* of the Democratic party joined with the Whigs to reject the treaty.

Immediately after their accession to power the Democratic party reëstablished the Sub-Treasury system and repealed the protective tariff of 1842, and enacted in its place the revenue tariff of 1846, and also annexed Texas and admitted it into the Union, which gave rise to the Mexican war.

The country acquiesced in the financial policy adopted by the Democratic party in 1846, since which time the tariff has ceased to be a party question, the great majority of both parties now acquiescing substantially in the *revenue principle* in antagonism to the *protective policy*, and the Sub-Treasury having worked so satisfactorily as to receive the support of all parties under every administration which has succeeded, without opposition or complaint. *Here ends the financial chapter in our history ! !*

PROHIBITION OF THE AFRICAN SLAVE TRADE.

Art. I., *Section* 9, *Clause* 1. "The migration or importation of such persons as any of the States now existing shall think proper to admit, shall not be prohibited by the Congress prior to the year one thousand eight hundred and eight, but a tax or duty may be imposed on such importation not exceeding ten dollars for each person."

THE section of the Constitution authorizing the prohibition of the African slave trade after the year 1808, had its origin in a disagreement between the delegates in the convention which framed the Constitution. One party, particularly the delegates of South Carolina and Georgia, demanded the instant and unconditional prohibition of the African slave trade on moral and religious grounds, while the delegates from the extreme South insisted that it was a legitimate commerce, involving no other considerations than those of a sound public policy, which each

State ought to be permitted to determine for itself. Each party adhered to its position resolutely, with the distinct avowal that they would maintain it at all hazards, until both became convinced that the convention must break up without forming a Constitution, and the Confederacy divide into two or more fractions, thus blotting out all the glories of the Revolution, and destroying its benefits, unless a compromise could be effected on the common ground of such mutual concessions as were necessary to preserve the Union, and independence of the States. Such a compromise was effected, and incorporated into the Constitution, by which *it was understood* that the slave trade should continue a legitimate commerce in those States which chose to sanction it, until the year 1808, from and after which time Congress might, and *would* prohibit it forever throughout the limits of America, and pass all laws necessary to make such prohibition effectual. This was the understanding with which this section was incorporated into the Constitution.

SUSPENSION OF THE WRIT OF HABEAS CORPUS.

Art. I., *Sec.* 9, *Clause* 2. "The privilege of the writ of Habeas Corpus shall not be suspended, unless when in cases of Rebellion or Invasion the public Safety may require it."

WE have to consider the suspension of the writ, the power of anybody to suspend, except the Congress, and then only under the circumstances described by the Constitution.

The most memorable case in our history of suspending the writ of habeas corpus without the authority of statute was in 1814, when General Jackson was in command of the Southwest division of the United States, and was engaged in repelling an invasion of the British army under the command of General Packenham. General Jackson established his headquarters in the city of New Orleans, where he found an immense number of foreigners (they had recently come into the Union, and were French and Spanish), who had no sympathy with the United States, and were either friendly to the British, or preparing to make terms with the enemy to save their property. General Jackson suspected, among others, a man by the name of Louelier with being a spy, and furnishing information to the British commander. Relying upon these suspicions, which he believed to be well founded, but without having legal evidence of the fact, and, having *to provide for all this, previously declared martial law*, he arrested and imprisoned him, and his supposed confederates.

Judge Hall, of the United States District Court, issued a writ of habeas corpus for the release of Louelier, and directed Jackson to bring him before the Court. To which Jackson replied by arresting the Judge, and sending him outside of the limits of the city, which he had previously declared to be under martial law.

About the same time General Jackson was informed and believed, that the Legislature of the State of Louisiana, then in session in the city of New Orleans, were about passing an act surrendering the city into the hands of the enemy; and in order to prevent such a result, he sent a detachment of troops to surround the Legislative Hall, and hold the members as prisoners in their own hall, cutting off all communication with anybody except himself. He then proceeded to meet the enemy, which he did, first on the night of the 23d of December, 1814, and, finally, on the 8th of January, 1815, won the final battle, by which the British army were routed and returned to their ships, peace having been previously signed in Europe, and news of the fact reaching New Orleans after the battle. General Jackson then withdrew his declaration of martial law, and restored the civil authorities. *He then delivered himself up to the court, and was fined one thousand dollars, which he immediately paid.*

Afterwards, while General Jackson was President of the United States, he would never permit any of his friends to propose an act of Congress for the remission of his fine; but after he retired from the Presidency such a proposition was introduced, from time to time, until it passed eventually, at the session of 1843, or 1844.

Pending the bill for the remission of the fine, the opponents of General Jackson opposed the measure, upon the ground that his declaration of martial law and imprisonment of the civil authorities was a violation of the Constitution of the

United States; consequently that it was the duty of Judge Hall to vindicate the dignity of his Court and the civil authorities by arresting and imprisoning him, and that the fine should not be refunded, for the reason that it would be licensing and sanctioning a violation of the Constitution, and cast a reflection upon the Court for having performed its solemn duty.

In reply, the friends of General Jackson had all admitted the violation of the Constitution and laws by the declaration of martial law, but justified the act upon the ground that it was necessary to save the city of New Orleans, and the State of Louisiana from the ravages of the enemy. This necessity was admitted by the other side, but still it was argued, that having violated the Constitution, he must bear the consequences, although governed by patriotic motives. I was the first man who denied that General Jackson violated the Constitution, by his declaration of martial law, and insisted that General Jackson having been charged under the Constitution and laws with the preservation of the city of New Orleans and the surrounding country from the assaults of the enemy, was clothed with all the power necessary to the performance of that duty; that by imposing a duty, the means necessary to its performance were included, and if the declaration of martial law was necessary and indispensable, as was admitted on all hands, *that necessity conferred the authority and limited its extent and duration. The authority went just so far as the necessity extended, and ceased when it ceased.*

John Quincy Adams, while he denied the necessity, admitted my argument, and though he voted against refunding the fine, he censured those who, believing in the necessity, also voted in the negative. The money was refunded.

Art. I., Sec. 9, Clause 5. "No tax or duty shall be laid on articles exported from any State."

For commercial purposes the whole United States are one State, or commercial district. They are not foreign to each other.

Art. I., Sec. 9, Clause 6. "No preference shall be given by any regulation of commerce or revenue to the ports of one State over those of another; nor shall vessels bound to, or from, one State, be obliged to enter, clear, or pay duties in another."

This clause means simply that duties shall not be imposed simply because the vessel goes across the State line, nor that on entering State ports the vessel may not be obliged to pay the same duties of tonnage, etc., as vessels of the State to which the ports belong. See in this connection—

Art. I., *Sec.* 10, *Clause* 3. "No State shall *without the consent of Congress*," etc.

Hence I hold that a duty may be imposed for river and harbor improvements, which question we will here consider, together with that of internal improvements.

INTERNAL IMPROVEMENTS.

RIVER AND HARBOR IMPROVEMENTS.

The advocates of a system of internal improvements, by the Federal Government, do not agree among themselves in respect to the clause of the Constitution which confers the power. Some contend that the power exists under the clause for "common defence and general welfare." The advocates of the power under this clause are again divided into those who claim it under the war power for the common defence, and who limit its exercise to such works as are necessary for the defence of the country, while others claim that Congress may make any road, canal, or other work of internal improvement which is for the general welfare of the United States. Others again derive the power from the clause which authorizes Congress "to establish post-offices and post-roads;" while the general opinion among those who advocate internal improvements by the General Government, and especially the friends of river and harbor improvements, claim to derive the power from the clause which authorizes Congress "to regulate commerce with foreign nations, and among the several States, and with the Indian tribes."

I, and others, contend that it is wiser and better to allow each State to improve its own rivers and harbors; that the "duty of tonnage" was inserted for this express purpose, and for that reason, *as asserted in debate at the time*, and the form originally was, "that the States reserve the power for imposing duties of tonnage." But it was suggested that this would interfere with the power of Congress to regulate commerce, which ought to be *exclusive*, and it was then modified, as in the Constitution, so as to read, "*without the consent of Congress*," so that the States might not conflict with the general power of Congress, *but that with the consent of Congress*, they might lay duties of tonnage.

It is generally conceded now that under the provision to provide for the general defence, Congress may construct such military works and roads as *are necessary for that purpose*, and are *made for that purpose*, but must not, under *pretence of general defence*, make artificial channels of commerce for *commercial, and not military purposes.* The general welfare power is generally abandoned. Post-offices and post-roads are generally construed now, to confer the right to designate the route over which the mail shall go, *but not to make the road.* Under the power to regulate commerce a majority believe that Congress may improve rivers and harbors, but *they doubt the expediency.* A majority *do not yet believe* that the States may do so by means of duties.

Calhoun spent the greater portion of his life in advocating internal improvements. He proposed *to build an arched covered road* from Buffalo to New Orleans. He was a visionary! No Statesman!

On the subject of internal improvements, I refer you to the report of J. C. Calhoun, as Secretary of War under Mr. Monroe, and the message of Mr. Monroe in favor of a system of internal improvements under the General Government. See also the veto messages of General Jackson upon the Maysville road bill, in Kentucky, and upon the Wabash River improvement bill; the veto message of President Polk upon the River and Harbor Improvement bill; report of J. C. Calhoun to the Memphis Convention, upon the improvement of the Western rivers, in which he called them "inland seas," and to the history of the internal improvement question in Wheeler's "Biographical Dictionary of Congress."

In the beginning this question of internal improvements was as much a Southern as a Northern one. In later periods the Democratic party of the South opposed it, *except where members had works of improvement in their own districts.* The Whig party generally, North and South, were for the system, and the Republicans, in 1856, endorsed the River and Harbor improvement system.

I believe the power to improve navigation and natural channels to exist, but not to construct artificial ones. It has been held by the Supreme Court that the Federal Government, under the Constitution, by virtue of the power to regulate commerce, has jurisdiction over all navigable waters, whether *within* the States, or *between*, or upon the high seas. Hence the right to improve that navigation does not conflict with the reserved rights of the States, so long as it is confined within the acknowledged jurisdiction of the United States. But the right to construct canals and railroads, and other artificial channels of commerce, within the limits of the several States, presupposes the right to exercise jurisdiction over the works thus constructed, which involves an invasion of the jurisdiction and reserved rights of the States.

The Federal Government has exercised legislative jurisdiction over the navigable waters between and within the States in a variety of cases, such as the passage of laws regulating steamboats upon the rivers and lakes, as well as upon tidewater, even including ferry-boats, and providing for the inspection of their boilers, and granting certificates by Federal agents of their capacity and soundness. This shows that the Legislative Department recognize this jurisdiction, as well as the Judiciary.

The common law had its origin in England. It grew up from custom and immemorial usage. It was a principle of the common law that the maritime jurisdiction extended only so far as the tide ebbs and flows, because beyond that, they in England had no rivers or lakes which were navigable, and therefore no commerce. The principle of law, thus, merely conformed to the *fact*. With us, we have lakes and rivers navigable beyond the ebb and flow of the tide, and while we have adopted the common law, the Court has held that we may extend the jurisdiction and legislate. We have legislated for rivers and lakes beyond the ebb and flow of the tide, though we have not extended admiralty and maritime jurisdiction. We thus conform to the reality, the principle, and not the name and the fact of the English common law.

ARTICLE SECOND.

OF THE EXECUTIVE POWER.

The Convention had once agreed to fix the Presidential term of office for seven years, and ineligible. It was also proposed for life, for fifteen or twenty years, and afterwards changed to four years, and not made ineligible. General Washington fixed the principle of not more than two terms, and it has obtained the force of law.

POWER OF THE PRESIDENT TO MAKE REMOVALS AND TO FILL VACANCIES.

Nothing said in the Constitution. In the early years of the Government it was decided, and has since been held, that the power of appointment involves the power of removal, in all cases where the tenure of office is not prescribed in the Constitution. This was so fixed by discussion in the first Congress of 1789, 1790, or 1791, in establishing some of the

Departments of the Government. It has also been held, and universally acquiesced in, that in cases where the appointment can only be made with the advice and consent of the Senate, the removal can be made by the President alone. The reason of this decision is not apparent, but practice and universal acquiescence have given it the force of law. Under the power to fill vacancies during the recess of the Senate, it has been held that the President cannot make an original appointment to an office which has been created by law but never filled. The commission the President gives during the recess of the Senate does not expire until the end of the next session, so that if on assembling the Senate do not confirm, he can wait until the end of their session, and then reappoint; the person appointed remaining in the mean time in the full and legal exercise of his office. This course was pursued by General Jackson when the Senate refused to confirm some of his appointments.

ARTICLE THIRD.

OF THE JUDICIAL POWER.

Section 2. "The judicial power shall extend to all cases of admiralty and maritime jurisdiction."

To those cases only which were then known to the common and statute law, or to those also which should be subsequently added by law?

The better opinion is, that Congress may define what cases come within admiralty and maritime jurisdiction, but under this clause ought to confine themselves to such cases as are of that nature.

"To controversies between citizens of different States."

The Court has made a decision which it will be obliged to reverse, namely, that a citizen of a Territory is not a citizen of a State within the meaning of this clause. But they have decided that within the clause providing for uniform taxation he is a citizen of a State; that he is for taxation but not for judicial purposes. They have got to reverse this decision.

"The citizens of each State shall be entitled to all privileges and immunities of citizens in the several States."

This clause is confined to civil rights, and does not extend to political privileges. The word "State" includes Territory.

"No person held to service or labor in one State, under the laws thereof, escaping into another, shall, in consequence of any law or regulation therein, be discharged from such service or labor, but shall be delivered up on claim of the party to whom such service or labor may be due."

This clause defines who may be slaves, what a slave is, where he may exist as such, and by what authority. In a State only and under the laws thereof, and not under the Constitution of the United States. By virtue of State authority, not Federal. No person can be a slave under any other circumstances. The word State includes Territory, and every other political community recognized by law, and existing under the Constitution of the United States.

"New States may be admitted by the Congress into this Union."

"New States" means what are now called Territories. According to present phraseology it would read, "Territories may be admitted," in the same sense in which Mr. Jefferson used it in his plan of 1784, and in which Mr. Madison used it in the Convention, in his proposition of powers to be added.

The Dred Scott case decides that this is the only clause of the Constitution which authorizes the enlargement of the boundaries of the United States, and the acquisition of territory, for the purpose of making new States. That the power to acquire, includes the power to apply the territory to the purposes for which it was acquired, and to institute governments for the inhabitants living therein, and that these powers are all embraced within the clause authorizing Congress to admit new States. That this clause authorizes the acquisition of territory for the purpose of making new States, which is not in a condition at the time to be admitted into the Union, but may be retained until it has the requisite population, and is in a condition to be admitted.

The requisite population is not fixed by the Constitution. The rule of Mr. Jefferson, in his plan of 1784, was, that the population of the new State to be admitted should be equal to that of the smallest of the original thirteen. The rule now generally considered correct is, that it should contain a population equal to that requisite for members of Congress under the existing ratio.

The first time that the doctrine was advanced, that the right to acquire territory was included within the power to admit new States, was in a speech made by me on the annexation of Texas; and the first time the doctrine was advanced that the power to establish territorial governments was likewise so included, was in a report made by me as chairman of the Committee on Territories, in Senate of the United States, on the 12th day of March, 1856. The general impression had previously been that the power to institute territorial governments was included within the power "to dispose of and make all needful rules and regulations respecting the territory or other property belonging to the United States," which has been exploded by the Supreme Court in the Dred Scott case, and the power traced to the provision to admit new States. The Supreme Court had previously recognized, or rather intimated, but not expressly decided, the latter principle; and some laughed at my report of 1856.

"The Congress shall have power to dispose of and make all needful rules and regulations respecting the territory or other property belonging to the United States; and nothing in this Constitution shall be so construed as to prejudice any claims of the United States, or of any particular State."

This clause relates to property, and not to persons or communities. Its original form, as introduced by Mr. Madison in the Convention, was, "Congress shall have power to dispose of the waste and unappropriated lands of the United States." It was referred, in this form, to the committee of detail, to be revised and incorporated into the Constitution. The committee of detail changed "lands" into "territory," and added "other property," so that Congress should have the same power to dispose of the old ships, munitions of war, and every other description of property belonging to the United States, which was no longer needed for public use. The committee also added the right to make "needful rules and regulations," in order that Congress might protect and regulate all such property until it was disposed of. The history of this power clearly shows that it relates to property, and not to persons or communities.

In the Dred Scott case, the Supreme Court say that this clause was confined in its operation to the territory which the United States then owned at the time of the adoption of the Constitution, and has no force in Florida, the Louisiana purchase, or the Mexican or any other territory subsequently acquired. This is clearly an error, for unless the clause is in force in all the new Territories and States acquired since the adoption of the Constitution, Congress would have no power to provide for the surveys and sales of the public lands, or for the appointment of land offices, and the issuing of land patents, nor could Congress authorize the sale of military sites and other property not needed for public uses.

HISTORY OF THE ACQUISITIONS OF TERRITORY BY THE UNITED STATES.

THE LOUISIANA PURCHASE.

THE first foreign territory acquired by the United States is known as the Louisiana Purchase. It was purchased of France in 1803, and comprises the whole country west of the Mississippi, as far as the Rocky Mountains, and, taken in connection with the explorations of Lewis and Clarke, was one of the sources of our claim to Oregon.

When Mr. Jefferson instructed our ministers, Monroe and Pinckney, to acquire from Napoleon, then First Consul, a tract of country near the mouth of the Mississippi River, they were only authorized to purchase that portion lying east of the Mississippi River, and known as the Island of New Orleans, being bounded by the Gulf of Mexico, the Mississippi, the Iberville River, or Pass Manchac, as now called, and Lakes Ponchartrain and Borgne.

When our ministers made the proposition to Napoleon, he refused to sell the Island of New Orleans by itself, on any terms, but told them that they could have the whole of the province of Louisiana. They replied that their instructions limited them to the country east of the Mississippi, as the United States only desired the free navigation of that river, and possession of one of its banks, in order to secure that right. Napoleon persisted in his refusal to sell a part, but insisted upon their taking the whole, and it is said that he subsequently gave as a reason, that England and the other European powers were forming a new combination against him, and that the British navy were about to sail against Louisiana, at a time when he had no means to prevent its capture; that he was reduced to the alternative of permitting that vast province to be captured by his most formidable enemy, or to transfer it to the United States upon whatever terms they would accept it, adding, whatever nation held the Valley of the Mississippi, would eventually be the most powerful on earth, and that, consequently, he preferred that a friendly nation should possess it, instead of the national, implacable enemy of France.

Monroe and Pinckney took the responsibility of making the treaty for the whole country, without authority from the Government; and when it was presented to Mr. Jefferson, he hesitated in accepting it, upon the ground that there was no authority in the Constitution for the acquisition of foreign territory; and while he was willing to take the responsibility of acquiring a small district, which was necessary for the common defence, as well as the navigation of the Mississippi, which was the channel of commerce for at least one-half of the Republic, he doubted whether he ought to accept a grant of such gigantic proportions, which, when subdivided and formed into States, would change the character of the entire Confederacy. When he determined to accept the provisions of the treaty, he still hesitated whether he should not first submit the question to the several States, in the form of a proposition to amend the Constitution for that purpose. At last he gave his own consent to accept the treaty, and send it to the Senate for ratification.

This acquisition of territory became a partisan issue between the Federal and Republican parties of that day—the former opposing, and the latter sustaining. The Senate ratified the treaty by the constitutional majority, and Congress immediately passed a law authorizing the President to accept the possession of the territory, and to preserve order therein, and protect the inhabitants in their rights of person, property, and religion, until a regular territorial government should be established.

In 1805 so much of the Louisiana purchase as is embraced within the present State of Louisiana, was organized into a Territory, under the title and style of the Territory of Orleans, and the provisions of the Ordinance of 1787, for the government of the territory northwest of the Ohio River, with the exception of the Sixth Article, prohibiting slavery, were adopted as the basis of that government. The residue of the purchase, including the present States of Arkansas, Missouri, Iowa, the greater part of Minnesota, the Territories of Kansas and Nebraska, and what is known as the Dakota country, was formed into a separate Territory, under the name of the Territory of Louisiana. In 1812 the Territory of Orleans was admitted into the Union, under the name of the State of Louisiana, and the name of the Territory of Louisiana was changed to that of Missouri.

ACQUISITION OF FLORIDA AND PARTS OF ALABAMA, MISSISSIPPI, AND LOUISIANA.

In 1811 Congress in secret session passed an act, in vague and doubtful terms, to authorize the President of the United States, in certain contingencies, to take possession of a district of country south of the thirty-first parallel of latitude, and on the east of the Mississippi and Iberville Rivers, having reference to that portion of Alabama and Mississippi which fronts on the Gulf of Mexico, and so much of the State of Louisiana (I speak of the present State) as was not included within the Louisiana purchase, and which country was at the time not in the actual possession of any civilized power, although claimed by Spain as part of the Floridas, and upon which several lawless communities were residing; some deriving their titles from Spanish, and others from English grants, made while England was in temporary occupation of Florida, while the greater portion of them held by no other title than actual possession.

Under this act Mr. Madison fitted out an expedition on the Ohio River, which floated down the Mississippi, and took possession of the country, part of which was subsequently annexed to the State of

Louisiana, and the residue was incorporated into the States of Mississippi and Alabama, by which those States were extended to the Gulf.

FLORIDA, OREGON, AND TEXAS, AND THE MEXICAN WAR, CALIFORNIA, AND NEW MEXICO.

In 1819 a treaty was made between the United States and Spain for the acquisition of the Floridas, which was ratified in this country the same year, and rejected by Spain, but was subsequently reconsidered and ratified by Spain in 1821, by which our title to Florida takes effect from the date of the treaty in 1819. Florida was immediately organized into a Territory, and governed herself in that condition until 1838, when she called a convention, framed a Constitution, and applied for admission into the Union. Congress took no notice of this application, leaving Florida under the territorial government until 1845, when the State was admitted under the Constitution adopted in 1838.

In the treaty of 1819, for the acquisition of Florida, was a provision establishing and defining the boundaries between the Spanish Mexican provinces and the United States, by a line up the Sabine River; thence due north to the Red River; thence up the Red River to a point where the one hundredth degree of longitude, west from Greenwich, crossed the same; thence due north on said meridian to the Arkansas River; thence up the Arkansas to its source; thence due north to the forty-second parallel of latitude; thence due west on said parallel to the Pacific Ocean or South Sea—thus ceding to Spain, in part payment for Florida, the claim of the United States, which had been previously supposed to be valid, to the country between the Sabine and Rio Grande, and which was afterwards formed into the Republic of Texas.

By the resolutions of the Democratic National Convention at Baltimore in 1844, when Mr. Polk was nominated for the Presidency, the Democratic party declared the *re*-annexation of Texas, and the *re*-occupation of Oregon, to be objects which they intended to accomplish in the event of success. Much comment and ridicule has been indulged in, because of the RE-annexation and RE-occupation. By the *re*-annexation of Texas, reference was had to the fact that it was originally embraced within the French province of Louisiana, and consequently became the property of the United States, by virtue of the treaty of 1803, by which that province was acquired, and was subsequently ceded to Spain by the Florida treaty of 1819. By the *re*-occupation of Oregon, reference was had to the first discovery and navigation of the Columbia River, in or about the year 1789, by Captain Grey, of Boston, with his ship Columbia, and to the exploration of Lewis and Clarke in the year 1805, and to the settlements and establishments of John Jacob Astor and his associates, under the protection and authority of the United States, in the years 1809, 1810, 1811, 1812, and 1813.

During the war of 1812, a British ship-of-war entered the Columbia River and captured Astoria, hauled down the American flag, raised the British, and named the post Fort George, and held exclusive possession of the country until after the treaty of peace.

In 1818 a treaty was formed between the United States and Great Britain in respect to Oregon, by which it was agreed that the disputed title and boundary to the country should remain in abeyance, and that neither party would make any permanent settlements or establishments within the same during the period of the treaty, which was for twenty years, and until abolished.

Notwithstanding the stipulations of this treaty, the Hudson Bay Company kept up their settlements throughout the valley of the Columbia, and established new ones, under the protection of British laws, and, in fact, held the actual occupation of the country, with the exception of the Wilhamette Valley, in which American settlements commenced forming about 1832 or 1833, and gradually increased from that period. The American Government did not feel itself at liberty, under the existing stipulations of the treaty, to extend the protection of our laws over the American settlements; and the American citizens finding themselves without government or protection, established a provisional government for themselves, upon the principle of *popular sovereignty*, composed of executive, legislative, and judicial departments, after the model of our State governments. The inhabitants lived peaceably and prosperously under this provisional government, maintaining order and preserving friendly relations with the Indians, until the month of August, 1848, when Congress organized the territorial government of Oregon, notice having been previously given to Great Britain for the termination of the treaty of joint occupation, as it was usually called, but more properly of *non*-occupation; and a treaty of settlement and boundaries having been made in 1846 between Great Britain and the United States, by which the forty-ninth parallel of latitude was made the permanent boundary between the two countries, Great Britain ceding all claims south, and the United States all claims north of that line.

This was an exciting controversy in our domestic politics. Polk had been pledged to fifty-four, forty. I proposed to institute a territorial government for Oregon without defining the boundaries or accepting any line; and as *our* settlements were *agricultural*, and the British were *fur-traders, we would have squatted them out.* Vancouver's Island, with excellent harbors, well timbered, good soil and climate, abounding in coal, and therefore an excellent coal depot for us on the Pacific, and possessing an area as large as that of Great Britain, was given up by us. Polk, to avoid the ruin of the Democratic party, precipitated the country into the Mexican war, thus avoiding and distracting attention. The British have organized that island, and the shores opposite, into British Columbia, and the gold discovered there recently lies ten miles on the other side of the line, and in the British territory. I had prepared a bill, according to my plan, read it to Mr. Polk, and he had assented to it, and it was about to pass the Senate, when he and his whole cabinet came down, and it was barely defeated on the ground that it would bring on a war with Great Britain.

In 1852 Oregon Territory was divided by a line commencing in the Pacific Ocean, and running up the main channel of the Columbia River to a point where the forty-sixth parallel of north latitude crossed the same, above the Cascades; thence due east on said parallel to the summit of the Rocky Mountains; and all between that line and the British possessions was organized into a territory under the name of Washington Territory. In 1857 and 1858 the people of Oregon Territory called a convention, under a law of their Legislature, and formed a State government, embracing the west half of Oregon Territory, and applied for admission into the Union, and were admitted at the session of Congress in 1859; and at the same time the east half was added, and incorporated within the Territory of Washington, until Congress should otherwise provide.

After the election of Mr. Polk, in 1844, and before his inauguration as President, Congress passed a joint resolution, making propositions to the Republic of Texas for her annexation to the United States, with the condition that she should be admitted into the Union as *one* State, with the privilege of forming *not exceeding four* other States, making five in all, out of the said State of Texas; and the further condition that such of these States as should be situated south of the line of thirty-six degrees thirty minutes, known as the Missouri Compromise line, should be admitted into the Union with or without slavery, as each State should determine for itself; and the State or States which should be formed out of the State of Texas, north of said line, should forever prohibit slavery. Texas agreed to these propositions, and became annexed to the United States in 1845; and in December of that year a law was passed, declaring the State of Texas to be one of the States of the Union, on an equal footing with the original States.

The Republic of Mexico, still claiming Texas as a portion of that Republic, to which she had never relinquished her title, considered and treated the act of the United States, in annexing and taking possession of Texas, as an act of war against that Republic, and accordingly marched her armies across the Rio Grande, within the limits of Texas, for the purpose of reconquering and occupying the country. In anticipation of this movement on the part of Mexico, President Polk had ordered a detachment of the American army, under the command of General Taylor, into the western portion of Texas. General Taylor landed and established his headquarters at Corpus Christi, near the mouth of the Neuces River, which was by some considered the western boundary of Texas, instead of the Rio Grande. After remaining some time (several months) at Corpus Christi, General Taylor took up his line of march for the Rio Grande, and established his headquarters at Point Isabel, a few miles from that river.

On the 8th of May, 1846, the two armies came in collision, the attack being made by the Mexicans at Palo Alto, where they were defeated and routed; and the next day, May 9th, another battle was fought and another victory won at Resaca de la Palma, still nearer to the Rio Grande. On the 13th of May, after these battles had been fought, but before the fact was known at Washington—although information had been received that the Mexicans had crossed the Rio Grande, and killed several Americans, who were detached from the main army as scouting parties, and were preparing with superior force to attack the American army—Congress passed a law with a preamble, reciting, "whereas *war exists* by the acts of Mexico," proceeded to appropriate men and money for the vigorous prosecution of the war.

The war was sustained by the Democratic party with almost entire unanimity, and was opposed bitterly by a large portion of the Whigs, particularly that section of the party which cherished anti-slavery proclivities.

By the treaty of peace, February 2d, 1848, we acquired the Mexican provinces of New Mexico and California, and paid for them $15,000,000, three and a quarter of which were to be applied by this Government to the payment of such claims as should be adjudged by a joint commission, and which citizens of the United States might have against the Republic of Mexico for previous wrongs. By this treaty a new boundary was fixed between the United States and Mexico, beginning at a point north of the Rio Grande River, instead of the Sabine, as had been previously fixed, and running up the Rio Grande to El Paso, which was near the thirty-second parallel of latitude, thence west to the head of the Gila River, thence down the Gila to its junction with the Colorado, thence in a direct line to the Pacific, to a point two or three leagues south of San Diego; by which boundary Mexico surrendered her claim to the whole of Texas, and ten degrees of latitude, including California and New Mexico.

HISTORY OF THE COMPROMISE OF 1820, OR THE MISSOURI COMPROMISE.

THE ADMISSION OF THE STATE INTO THE UNION.

In 1819 the people of the Territory of Missouri made application to Congress for permission to form a State government, preparatory to admission into the Union, with boundaries substantially the same as those defining the present State of Missouri, the variation consisting in the omission to include within the proposed State the district since known as the Platte country, which lay on the northeast side of the Missouri River and west of the limits of the State, and which, by an act of Congress in 1835 or 1836, was annexed and included within the limits of the State, and now comprises seven of its wealthiest counties. It was proposed at the same time that Congress should grant authority to the people of Missouri to form a State government; also to organize the country between the State of Louisiana and the proposed State of Missouri into the Territory of Arkansas. To each of these bills an amendment was proposed, that the said State might be admitted and the territory organized, on the express condition that neither slavery nor involuntary servitude should ever exist therein, except for crime. The proposition to prohibit slavery was not confined to the territory while it should remain in that condition, but provided that there should be a clause in the Constitution of the State of Missouri expressly prohibiting slavery, as a condition of her admission.

This proposition was sternly resisted by the entire South, and by a majority of the Republican or Democratic party throughout the country; but still only a few members from the North could be found who were willing to risk their popularity at home by voting against the Missouri restriction. A majority of the House of Representatives adopted the restriction, which the Senate rejected, and thus the bill for the formation of a State government for Missouri, and the organization of the Territory of Arkansas, was defeated at that session.

At the next session the controversy was renewed with increased excitement and great bitterness; the House of Representatives insisting upon the restriction, and the Senate rejecting the same. After several disagreements between the House and the Senate on this point, a compromise was proposed by Jesse B. Thomas, a Senator from the State of Illinois, by which it was provided that the people of Missouri might proceed to form their Constitution and State government preparatory to their admission into the Union on an equal footing with the original States, and that slavery should be forever prohibited in so much of the Louisiana purchase as was situated north of the parallel of thirty-six degrees thirty minutes, and not included within the limits of the proposed State. In this form the bill passed, and became a law on the 6th of March, 1820. In the month of June of that year, the people of Missouri assembled in convention and framed a Constitution and State government, recognizing and protecting African slaves, and, at the opening of the session in December of that year, presented the same to Congress, for acceptance and admission into the Union. The Senate passed the bill for the admission of the State, to which the House added an amendment, providing a fundamental condition to be first performed, that the State of Missouri should change her Constitution, and insert a clause therein prohibiting slavery. The Senate rejected the amendment, the House insisted upon it, and thus the question of admission, for the time, fell by the disagreement of the two houses.

By this time the excitement and sectional strife had become so intense that the country became alarmed for the consequences. At this stage of the proceedings, Mr. Clay, of Kentucky, proposed the appointment of a joint committee of the two houses, with the view to some fair and just compromise of their differences. A committee was appointed, and, after free conference, agreed upon a compromise, which provided, in substance, that the State of Missouri should be, and is hereby, admitted into the Union on the fundamental condition that the said State should never construe or execute certain provisions of the Constitution of Missouri (naming them), which related to the rights of free negroes, in such a manner as to violate the provisions of the Constitution of the United States!!! and that so soon as the State of Missouri should faithfully comply with the aforesaid fundamental condition, and should present authentic and satisfactory evidence thereof to the President of the United States, it should be his duty to issue his proclamation, declaring said State of Missouri to be admitted into the Union on an equal footing with the original States.

The joint committee reported the compromise to their respective houses. It was concurred in, and became a law on the 2d day of March, 1821.

In pursuance of this joint resolution of compromise, the Legislature of Missouri assembled in the month of June 1821, and proceeded to consider the terms and conditions upon which Congress proposed to admit them into the Union. After mature deliberation a *public and irrevocable* act was proposed by the late Senator Geyer of Missouri, and adopted by the Legislature in due form, by which, after setting out the terms of the joint resolution of Congress, it is declared, that whereas Congress has prescribed these terms as the only condition on which the State of Missouri can be admitted into the Union on an equal footing with the original States, and whereas the said terms are in palpable violation of the Constitution of the United States, and grossly insulting to the people of the State, and such as Congress had no right to pass, and as the people of the State ought not to accede to; and whereas the people of Missouri do not intend to respect and be bound by the said conditions, or to acknowledge the right of Congress to impose them, but inasmuch as we cannot obtain our constitutional rights in any other mode than by giving our assent to the same, with the protest that we shall not respect them—therefore be it known, that we, the people of Missouri, do declare by this fundamental and irrevocable act, etc., etc.!!! This act of Missouri, duly authenticated, was presented to President Monroe as the basis for his proclamation. On the 10th of August, 1821, he issued his proclamation, declaring, that whereas Congress had passed such a resolution admitting Missouri, on a fundamental condition, and whereas Missouri *had complied*, therefore I, James Monroe, do declare and admit the State as one of the States of the Union.

Remark, that Monroe did not publish the act of the Missouri Legislature!!

It was all a burlesque! Clay's account of it was that they met one Sunday, took some brandy, threw dust in their eyes, and gave them an excuse *to back down*. Thus vanishes Clay's Compromise of 1820. He declared that he would not vote for the restriction as to slavery, with which he had nothing to do. *It came from Illinois, and Illinois repealed it!*

"THE WILMOT PROVISO AND THE COMPROMISE OF 1850."

PENDING the war, when, in August, 1846, the President asked for additional appropriations, and for $2,000,000 to be used in negotiating a treaty of peace, and as the first instalments of any sums that we might give for the cession of territory, Mr. *Wilmot*, of Pennsylvania, offered a *proviso* to the bill appropriating $2,000,000, to the effect that any treaty or compact by which territory should be acquired, should contain a stipulation that neither slavery nor involuntary servitude should ever exist in the territory thus to be ceded. This was the original of what is known as the *Wilmot Proviso.*

The proviso was adopted in the House of Representatives as an amendment to the bill; and, as thus amended, it was sent for concurrence to the Senate, where it was rejected because of the proviso, and the appropriation was defeated.

The war still went on, and at the next session the President recommended Congress to appropriate $3,000,000 for the purpose of enabling him to make peace and to procure the cession of territory. The House of Representatives passed a bill appropriating $3,000,000, with the Wilmot Proviso attached, and sent it to the Senate, where, by a protracted discussion on the last day of the short session, the bill failed for the want of time, and in consequence of the opposition of the Senate to the proviso.

After peace was made, and the additional territory acquired, the slavery question again became a disturbing element in our politics. The large majority of the Northern States demanded that the Wilmot Proviso should be attached to any bill for the organization of territorial governments, while the entire South, with many Northern Democrats, resisted this claim. The two houses of Congress being unable to agree on this question, it became an issue in the Presidential election of 1848, and secured the election of General Taylor, the Whig candidate, over General Cass, the Democratic candidate, by dividing the Democratic party in the Northern States, and thus enabling the Whigs to succeed—Martin Van Buren, Democrat, and C. F.

Adams, Whig, having accepted the nomination from a Freesoil Convention held at Buffalo in 1848, and running upon a platform pledging its candidates and supporters to prohibit slavery, by an act of Congress, in all the Territories of the United States, and in the dockyards, forts, and arsenals, and wherever else Congress had exclusive jurisdiction. Cass ran upon the issue of *non-intervention* by Congress with slavery in the Territories, as explained in his celebrated letter to A. O. P. Nicholson, of Tennessee, and known as the *Nicholson Letter*. The Whig National Convention, which nominated General Taylor, made no platform, leaving the party free to take such course as they should see proper in their several State conventions, with the understanding, and which was in fact the case, that in the free States they would pledge their party to the Wilmot Proviso, and in the slaveholding they would repudiate it, and deny that their candidate was committed to it, and that *he, meanwhile, should express no opinion upon the subject*.

General Taylor was elected President, but his election, instead of quieting the agitation upon the slavery question, aggravated the evil, and increased the excitement. Nearly all the Northern States then, by resolutions in their several Legislatures, demanded the application of the Wilmot Proviso to all the Territories; while the Southern States, by the resolutions of their Legislatures, denounced the measure as unconstitutional, violative of their rights, and derogatory to their character as equal and independent members of the Confederacy. At the session of Congress which met in December, 1848, immediately succeeding the Presidential election, no action was taken for the organization of the new Territories. Political parties became arrayed upon the distinct issue of the prohibition of slavery by Congress in all the Territories, and upon the question of slavery generally, which became the engrossing question in the Congressional elections, which took place during the recess, and by which the excitement was greatly increased, and the country arrayed in two hostile sections. When Congress assembled in December, 1849, the whole country had become alarmed for the peace and safety of the Union. Mr. Clay, who had for years been in private life, consented to return to the United States Senate, and contribute his best efforts to the restoration of peace, and the adjustment of the sectional dispute upon some fair basis.

Upon the 29th of January, 1850, Mr. Clay introduced a series of resolutions, with the hope that they would become the basis of such legislation as would settle the matters in dispute. Pending the discussion of these resolutions, Mr. Douglas, as chairman of the Committee on Territories, on the 25th of March, reported two bills, the one for the admission of California as a State, and the other for the organization of the Territories of Utah and New Mexico, and the adjustment of the disputed boundary with Texas. On the 19th of April Senator Foote, of Mississippi, proposed the appointment of a committee of thirteen, to which the propositions and matters in dispute touching the slavery question, should be referred. The committee was appointed, and Clay made chairman.

On the 8th of May, Mr. Clay, from the Committee of Thirteen, made an elaborate report covering all the points in dispute, accompanied by a bill. By reference to the bill as it now appears on the files of the Senate, it will be seen that it consists of the two printed bills previously reported from the Committee on Territories, by Mr. Douglas, with a wafer between them, and black lines drawn through the words, in the heading, "Mr. Douglas, from the Committee on Territories," and written with a pen. "Mr. Clay, from the Committee of Thirteen, made the following report." The only material change or amendment made in the Territorial bills, is found in that section which defines the powers of the Territorial Legislature. The bill, as reported by Mr. Douglas, provided that the power of the Territorial Legislature should extend to all rightful subjects of legislation, consistent with the Constitution, *without excepting African slavery;* while the bill, as modified by the Committee of Thirteen, conferred the same power on the Territorial Legislature, *with the exception of African slavery.* A debate immediately sprang up, upon the question whether the Territorial Legislature should have the power to introduce or to exclude African slavery. Mr. Davis, of Mississippi, proposed to amend the bill so that the Territorial Legislature should have the power to *protect*, but *not to exclude* slavery. Mr. Chase, of Ohio, proposed an amendment, in the form of a proviso, that the Territorial Legislature should not have the power to protect slavery, or recognize the right of property in man. Both of these amendments were rejected. Mr. Douglas moved to strike out the exception in respect to African slavery, so that the Territorial Legislature would have the same power over slavery as over all other rightful subjects of legislation. This amendment was, on the first trial, rejected; but when subsequently renewed by Mr.

Norris, of New Hampshire, at the suggestion of Mr. Douglas, it was adopted by a vote of thirty-three to nineteen. Norris was getting a little shaky, and I made him make the motion, to fix him.

Thus the bill reported by Mr. Clay was restored to the precise form in which it was previously reported by Mr. Douglas, and conferred upon the Territorial Legislature the same power over slavery as over all other rightful subjects of legislation. It is due to Mr. Clay to remark, that in an early portion of the debate, he stated to the Senate that the exception on African slavery was incorporated into the bill by the Committee of Thirteen, in opposition to his vote and contrary to his judgment, and that he voted to strike it out whenever the motion was made. Thus it will be seen that the compromise measures of 1850, so far as they related to the organization of the Territories, were founded upon the principle that the Territorial Legislature should determine the slavery question, and have the same power over it as over all other matters affecting their internal polity; and in this form the bill passed both houses, and became the law of the land, September 9, 1850.

The opponents of the compromises of 1850 at the North, as well as at the South, appealed to the people either to repeal or to resist the execution of these measures, for *opposite reasons*. *At the North,* because it was a total surrender of all Northern rights to the slavery interest, inasmuch as slavery had not been prohibited by Congress in the Territories, and because stringent measures had been provided for the rendition of fugitive slaves; while, *at the South,* it was insisted that there had been a total surrender of Southern rights by the admission of California into the Union, *with a prohibition of slavery in her Constitution,* and by leaving slave property in the Territories at the mercy of the Territorial Legislatures. *The friends of the compromise measures, however, stood firm, Whig and Democratic,* and insisted that their respective parties should endorse those measures in their national conventions for the nomination of Presidential candidates as a rule of action in the future. Accordingly, when the Whigs assembled in national convention at Baltimore in 1852, and nominated General Scott as their candidate for the Presidency, they declared in their platform that they approved and would carry out in good faith the compromise measures of 1850, "*in substance and in principle.*" The Democratic party assembled a few weeks afterwards at the same place, and after nominating

Franklin Pierce as their candidate for the Presidency, also adopted the same measures as a part of their creed, by a unanimous vote. Thus it will be seen that the two great political parties of the country stood upon the same platform, so far as the slavery question was involved, and that the principal point of controversy in that canvass was, which party could be most safely relied upon to carry those principles into effect in good faith. The fact that Mr. Seward was the violent opponent of President Fillmore, and the warm advocate of General Scott's nomination, gave the impression to the country that General Scott, if elected, would be in a great degree under the influence of the New York Senator, and thus tended to combine the conservative interests of the country against General Scott, and in favor of the Democratic nominee. Mr. Pierce was elected President in November, 1852, receiving the electoral vote of all the States, except Vermont, Massachusetts, Kentucky, and Tennessee, and an immense popular majority.

THE KANSAS-NEBRASKA BILL.

At the next meeting of Congress after the election of General Pierce, Mr. Douglas, as chairman of the Committee on Territories, reported the Kansas-Nebraska Bill, accompanied by a special report, in which he said, "that the object of the committee was to organize all Territories in the future upon the principles of the compromise measures of 1850. That these measures were intended to have a much broader and more enduring effect, than to merely adjust the disputed questions growing out of the acquisition of Mexican territory, *by prescribing certain great fundamental principles*, which, while they adjusted the existing difficulties, would prescribe rules of action in all future time, when new Territories were to be organized or new States to be admitted into the Union." The report then proceeded to show that the principle upon which the Territories of 1850 were organized was, that the slavery question should be banished from the halls of Congress and the political arena, and referred to the Territories and States who were immediately interested in the question, and alone responsible for its existence; and concluded, by saying "that the bill reported by the committee proposed to carry into effect these principles *in the precise language of the compromise measures of* 1850."

By reference to those sections of the Kansas-Nebraska Act which define the powers of the Territorial Legislature, it will be perceived that they *are* in the precise language of the acts of 1850, and confer upon the Territorial Legislature power over all rightful subjects of legislation, consistent with the Constitution, without excepting African slavery.

During the discussion of this measure it was suggested that the 8th section of the act of March 6, 1820, commonly called the Missouri Compromise, would deprive the people of the Territory, *while they remained in a Territorial condition* of the right to decide the slavery question, unless said 8th section should be repealed. In order to obviate this objection, and to allow the people the privilege of controlling this question, *while they remained in a Territorial condition*, the said restriction was declared inoperative and void, by an amendment which was incorporated into the bill, on the motion of Mr. Douglas, with these words in explanation of the object of the repeal: "*it being the true intent and meaning of this act, not to legislate slavery into any Territory or State, nor to exclude it therefrom, but to leave the people thereof perfectly free to form and regulate their domestic institutions in their own way, subject only to the Constitution of the United States.*" In this form, and with this intent, the Kansas-Nebraska Act became a law, by the approval of the President, on the 30th of May, 1854.

This bill and its author were principally *assailed* upon two points. First, that it was not necessary to renew slavery agitation, by the introduction of the measure; and secondly, that there was no necessity for the repeal of the Missouri restriction.

To the first objection *it was replied*, that there was a necessity for the organization of the Territory, which could no longer be denied or resisted. That Mr. Douglas, as early as the session of 1843, had introduced a bill to organize the Territory of Nebraska, for the purpose of opening the line of communication between the Mississippi Valley and our possessions on the Pacific Ocean, known as the Oregon country, and which was then under the operation of the treaty of joint occupation, or rather non-occupation, with England, and was rapidly passing into the exclusive possession of the British Hudson's Bay Fur Company, who were establishing posts at every prominent and commanding point in the country. That the Oregon Territory was, therefore, practically open to English emigrants, by ships, while it was closed to all emigration from our Western States by our Indian intercourse laws, which imposed a thousand dollars penalty, and six months' imprisonment, upon every American citizen who should be found within the Indian country which separated our settlements in the Mississippi or Missouri Valley from the Oregon Territory. That the desire for emigration in that direction was so great, that petitions were poured into Congress at every session for the organization of the Territory. Mr. Douglas renewed the introduction of his bill for the organization of Nebraska Territory, each session of Congress, from 1844 to 1854, a period of ten years, and while he had failed to secure the passage of the act, in consequence of the Mexican war intervening, and the slavery agitation which ensued, *no one had objected to it upon the ground that there was no necessity for the organization of the Territory.* During the discussions upon our Territorial questions during this period, Mr. Douglas often called attention to the fact that a line of policy had been adopted many years ago, and was being executed each year, which was entirely incompatible with the growth and development of our country. It had originated as early as the administration of Mr. Monroe, and had been continued by Mr. Adams, General Jackson, Mr. Van Buren, Harrison, and by Tyler, by which treaties had been made with the Indians to the east of the Mississippi River, for their removal to the country bordering upon the States west of the Mississippi or Missouri Rivers, with guaranties in said treaties that the country within which these Indians were located should never be embraced within any Territory or State, or subjected to the jurisdiction of either, so long as grass should grow and water should run. These Indian settlements, thus secured by treaty, commenced upon the northern borders of Texas, or Red River, and were continued from year to year westward, until, when in 1844, Mr. Douglas introduced his first Nebraska Bill, they had reached the Nebraska or Platte River, and the Secretary of War was then engaged in the very act of removing Indians from Iowa, and settling them in the valley of the Platte River, with similar guaranties of perpetuity, by which the road to Oregon was forever to be closed. It was the avowed object of this Indian policy to form an Indian barrier on the western borders of Arkansas, Missouri, and Iowa, by Indian settlements, secured in perpetuity by a compact, that the white settlements should never extend westward of that line. This policy originated in the jealousy, on the part of the Atlantic States, of the growth and expansion of the Mississippi Valley, which threatened in a few years to become the controlling power of the nation. Even Colonel Benton, of Missouri, who always claimed to be the champion of the West, made a speech, in which he erected the god Terminus upon the summit of the Rocky Mountains, facing eastward, and with uplifted hand, saying to Civilization and Christianity, "Thus far mayst thou go, and no farther!" and General Cass, while Secretary of War, was zealous in the execution of this policy. This restrictive system received its first check in 1844, by the introduction of the Nebraska Bill, which was served on the Secretary of War, by its author, on the day of its introduction, with a notice that Congress was about to organize the Territory, and therefore he must not locate any more Indians there. In consequence of this notice, the Secretary (by courtesy) suspended his operations until Congress should have an opportunity of acting upon the bill; and inasmuch as Congress failed to act that session, Mr. Douglas renewed his bill and notice to the Secretary each year, and thus prevented action for ten years, and until he could procure action on the bill. In the mean time the passion of the Western people for emigration had become so aroused, that they could be no longer restrained; and Colonel Benton, who was a candidate in Missouri for re-election to the Senate in 1852 and 1853, so far yielded to the popular clamor, as to advise the emigrants, who had assembled, in a force of fifteen or twenty thousand, on the western border of Missouri, carrying their tents and wagons, to invade the Territory and take possession, in defiance of the Indian intercourse laws, and of the authority of the Federal Government, which, if executed, must inevitably have precipitated an Indian war with all those tribes.

When this movement on the part of Colonel Benton became known at Washington, the President of the United States despatched the Commissioner of Indian Affairs to the scene of excitement, with orders to the commanding officer at Fort Leavenworth to use the United States army in resisting the invasion, if he could not succeed in restraining the emigrants by persuasion and remonstrances.

The Commissioner of Indian Affairs succeeded in procuring the agreement of the emigrants that they would encamp on the western borders of Missouri, until the end of the next session of Congress, in order to see if Congress would not in the mean time, by law, open the country to emigration. When Congress assembled at the session of 1853-'54, in view of this state of facts, Mr. Douglas renewed his Nebraska Act, which was modified, pending discussion, by dividing into two Territories, and became the Kansas-Nebraska Act. *From these facts you can draw your own conclusion, whether there was any necessity for the organization of the Territory and of Congressional action at that time.*

In regard to the second objection, it is proper to remark, that if the necessity for the organization of the Territories did in fact exist, it was right that they should be organized upon *sound constitutional principles;* and if the compromise measures of 1850 were a safe rule of action upon that subject, *as the country* in the Presidential election, and *both of the political parties* in their national conventions in 1852 had affirmed, then it was the duty of those to whom the power had been intrusted to frame the bills *in accordance with those principles.* There was another reason which had its due weight in the repeal of the Missouri restriction. The jealousies of the two great sections of the Union, North and South, had been fiercely excited by the slavery agitation. The Southern States would never consent to the opening of those Territories to settlement, so long as they were excluded by act of Congress from moving there and holding their slaves; and they had the power to prevent the opening of the country forever, inasmuch as it had been forever excluded by treaties with the Indians, which could not be changed or repealed except by a two-third vote in the Senate. But the South were willing to consent to remove the Indian restrictions, provided the North would at the same time remove the Missouri restriction, and thus throw the country open to settlement on equal terms by the people of the North and South, and leave the settlers at liberty to introduce or exclude slavery as they should think proper. This was true; but this power to defeat the Kansas-Nebraska Act by refusing to make new treaties, that is, repealing the old by consent of both parties, the Indians and the United States, was overlooked by *both parties*, or the Kansas-Nebraska Act might have been defeated. I saw this objection, and was often on the point of letting it slip, in debate, but as often checked myself. In the mean time commissioners were sent out, pending the Nebraska Act, to make new treaties. A clause in the act made it prospective, so as to await this result. The treaties were made and ratified by the Senate. Bell, of Tennessee, saw the objection, and alluded to it; but he did not portray or grasp it fully. I pretended not to be listening to his speech, but was terribly frightened, when, on the *last night* of the Kansas-Nebraska Bill he made his speech against it (having been previously pledged to vote for it), but at a time when the whole South was pledged to it, and would hardly *even listen to what he was saying.* In that speech, Bell, in substance, said that he did not blame the Senator from Illinois for the part he was acting on this occasion—that Senator understood what he was about. He had a grand scheme for the building up of a great Northwestern empire, which would in a few years be strong enough to govern the whole country. His scheme contemplated the extinction of the Indian title to a country large enough for ten or twelve new States, which under his guidance would soon be brought into the Union, to swell the power of his own section. "I repeat that I do not blame the Senator for the part he is acting; I only blame the South for allowing themselves to be used as his instruments, to carry out his grand scheme for his own section. It is said that the Romans were in the habit of conferring a civic crown upon every Roman consul who added a new province to the empire. If his section of the country shall prove as grateful as the Romans, he will be entitled to ten civic crowns in gratitude for his services."

Immediately after the Nebraska Bill was introduced, and before the clause was inserted in the bill repealing the Missouri Compromise, an appeal to the people was prepared and published by Messrs. Chase of Ohio, Sumner of Massachusetts, Seward of New York, Wade, Giddings, and other leading Freesoilers, in which they denounced the measure as an attempt to open the whole Northern country to slavery, and, in fact, to introduce slavery into a country large enough for fourteen States by act of Congress, and denouncing the author of it as a traitor to the cause of freedom, to the North, and to the whole country; and appealing to the friends of freedom, and to all who were opposed to the extension of slavery, to forget all former party distinctions, hold public meetings, denounce the measure and its author, send up petitions and remonstrances from every town and hamlet in the country, urge the Legislatures to send up instructions, and requesting the *preachers of the gospel* to denounce it in their pulpits, and all *religious men* to assemble in prayer-meetings and invoke the interposition of divine vengeance against those who should consummate such a damnable crime. This appeal to the *passions* of the people was prepared by its authors *secretly*, and after being agreed to *in caucus on the Sabbath day*, as appears from its date, was printed and sent to every portion of the country the day before the bill was to be taken up for discussion in the Senate.

On the next morning, a few minutes before Mr. Douglas was to make his opening speech in favor of the bill, Mr. Chase and Mr. Sumner came to his desk *and appealed to his courtesy* to postpone the discussion for one week, and *assigned as a reason* that they had *not had time to read the bill* and *understand its provisions*, acknowledging that it was their own fault and neglect that they had not done so, and therefore that they had no other claim to ask the postponement than the courtesy of the author of the measure. Mr. Douglas yielded to their appeal, and granted the postponement. Three or four days afterwards, he received by mail from Ohio a printed copy of this appeal, signed by Chase and Sumner, *and bearing date several days before he had granted the postponement,* which conduct he immediately denounced in open Senate. They had thus *lied*—had got *first* before the country, seeking thus *by fraud* to forestall public opinion. Mr. Douglas' friends had reproved him for granting the postponement. He replied to them that it was a fair measure, and that he intended to act fairly and honestly, and to let friends and opponents all equally have an opportunity to use their abilities, for and against the measure, understandingly.

In response to this appeal the wildest passions were aroused. Meetings were held, violent resolutions of denunciation were passed, sermons preached, violence urged to any extent necessary to defeat the measure. As a specimen of the tone of the anti-Nebraska press, the New York "Tribune" threatened, and justified the execution of the threat, that if the measure could not be defeated in any other mode, the capital should have been burned over the heads of the members, or blown up with powder. Mr. Douglas was burned and hung in effigy in every portion of the free States, sometimes in a hundred different places in the same night, and nearly every pulpit of the Protestant churches poured forth its denunciations and imprecations upon every man who should vote for the measure. A memorial was presented in the Senate, among many others of the same character, containing the signatures of three thousand and fifty clergymen protesting against the measure in the name of Almighty God, and imploring His vengeance upon the author.

When the bill passed, the Freesoil members of the two houses immediately organized themselves into an Emigrant Aid Association at the city of Washington, and urged the formation of other associations in each of the free States for the purpose of sending emigrants to Kansas. The Massachusetts Legislature incorporated an Emigrant Aid Society, with a capital of $5,000,000, and immediately proceeded to ship emigrants to Kansas, armed with Colt's pistols, a bowie knife, and a Bible. *All the troubles of the Territory grew out of this armed and forced emigration.* There would have been no trouble if emigration had been left to its natural causes and course. *What I say about armed emigrants is all true.* I have seen five hundred of them, armed, come off the ships at Chicago, and howl and groan before my own door, with bands around their hats inscribed "Freedom to Kansas, down with the traitors!" When I returned to Chicago I was met at Buffalo by a friend, who brought letters from other friends at Chicago, protesting against my return, and warning me that I would be inevitably killed if I did. I insisted upon going, and did so. I arrived there in the morning, went to my hotel, and after a few days, three or four, issued a notice of a speech to be made by me in front of North Market Hall. All the newspapers in the city denounced me, and published daily articles encouraging personal violence, reminding the people that in 1850, on the passage of the compromise measures, I had returned and succeeded in quelling an outbreak against those measures, and that this thing could not be done a second time. *Know-Nothingism* had, pending the Nebraska Bill, been organized in the United States for the first time, and in Chicago the anti-Nebraska men had organized into Know-Nothing lodges, and probably included within those lodges nine-tenths of all the men in the city. It was ascertained that they secretly determined and bound themselves by their oaths not to allow me to speak; and it is known that one of these thirty or forty lodges ordered by telegraph, and received by express from New York, the night before I was to speak, two hundred and fifty of Colt's revolvers. When the day arrived the flags were hung at half-mast on the shipping in the harbor, and for several hours before the time appointed all the church bells in the city were tolled, at which signal the mob assembled in a force of about ten thousand. I had forty or fifty men who pretended to be with me *privately*, but not half a dozen were so *openly;* they were all afraid. At the appointed hour I repaired to the meeting and went upon the stand, and was greeted by that unearthly yell taught and practised in the Know-Nothing lodges, a howl no man can imitate. I stood and looked at the mob until the howling ceased. When they ceased I commenced by saying, that "I appear before you to-night for the purpose of vindicating the provisions of the Kansas-Nebraska Act." Before the sentence was ended the howl began again. When it ceased I would begin, and as soon as I commenced it was renewed. At times I appealed to their pride, as the champions of free speech, for a hearing; the howling was renewed; at other times I would denounce them as a set of cowards who came armed with bowie knives and pistols to put down one man, unarmed—afraid to hear the truth spoken, lest there might be some honest men amongst them who would be convinced. At one time I got a hearing for ten or fifteen minutes, and was evidently making an impression upon the crowd, when there marched in from the outside a body of three or four hundred men with red shirts, dressed as sailors, and thoroughly armed, who moved through the crowd immediately in front of the stand, and then peremptorily ordered me to leave it. I stood and looked at them until they ceased yelling, and then denounced them and put them at defiance, and dared them to shoot at an unarmed man. The pistols began to fire all around the outside of the crowd, evidently into the air; eggs and stones were thrown at the stand, several of them hitting men that were near me, and for several hours this wild confusion and fury continued. The wonder is that amid that vast excited crowd no one was so far excited or maddened as to fire a ball at me. The stand was crowded with my enemies, reporters, and newspaper men, and this was undoubtedly my best protection. I stood upon the front of the stand, in the midst of that confusion, from eight o'clock in the evening until a quarter past twelve at night, when I suddenly drew my watch from my pocket and looked at it, in front of the crowd, and in a distinct tone of voice said, at an interval of silence, "It is now Sunday morning—I'll go to church, and you may go to hell!" and I retired amidst the uproar, got into my carriage and rode to my hotel. The crowd followed the carriage, and came near throwing it off the bridge into the river as we crossed; they had seized it for that purpose, and lifted it, but the driver whipped his horses violently, and dashed through and over them, and went to the Tremont House, where I retired to my room. The mob, at least five thousand, followed, and commenced their howls in Lake Street, fronting my room. The landlord begged me to leave the house, fearing they would burn it up, whereupon I raised my window, walked out on the balcony, took a good look at them, and told them that *the day would come when they would hear me,* and then bade them goodnight.

After the organization of the opposition societies in the South and North, for the purpose of peopling the Territory, with a view to control the first Legislature, President Pierce appointed Reeder, Governor of Kansas, who, instead of calling an election for the organization of the Territory, immediately after his appointment, and before these hired emigrants arrived there, waited until late in the fall, nearly a year, and ordered the election for the 29th of March, 1855, for the first Legislature, at a time in the winter when many of the Eastern emigrants had returned to their homes. They had established no homes in Kansas, had gone in the fall, and returned in the winter. Most of them had only gone to vote, and return the next day. A few days before the election large bodies of men could be seen marching from the various towns in Western Missouri to the Kansas border, and on the election day, and the day previous, they were crossing the Missouri River at all points into Kansas, in armed parties—some with cannon and baggage-wagons, and took possession of all the villages along the Missouri River, and penetrated to some distance into the interior, and *thus controlled the election.* When the returns of the election were made to Governor Reeder, protests were filed against giving the certificates from a majority of the election districts, on the ground of fraud, violence, and illegal election, leaving seven or eight districts uncontested where there were no such complaints of violence and fraud. Governor Reeder investigated the facts of each case before he granted the certificates, and in some instances granted certificates of election, and in other districts issued writs for new elections to take place in the month of May, 1855. At the election in May the same members were reëlected in a portion of the country, while in others different candidates were returned as elected, and they all received their certificates of election from the Governor.

The Governor then issued his proclamation for the Legislature to assemble at a town he and others had laid out upon the military reservation at Fort Riley, by the connivance of the commanding officer, who was one of the Governor's secret partners, and who was subsequently tried by court-martial and cashiered for his conduct. (The place was named, I believe, Pawnee, but see on this subject my report to the Senate of March 12, 1856.) When the Legislature assembled at Pawnee, they found no conveniences at Fort Riley, no houses to live in, with but one house in the place, and that without a floor, in which the Legislature was to assemble, while the cholera was raging at the fort, which was, in consequence, nearly abandoned. The members camped out on the ground, and in their wagons. The two houses organized by the election of their officers, and then proceeded to examine all the cases of contested election, deciding that the Governor had no authority to withhold the certificates in the first election, and to order a second, and hence confirmed in their seats all who were elected at the first election with but one exception, a Freesoiler. The Legislature then proceeded to remove the seat of Government to Shawnee Mission, where there was a settlement and buildings suitable for them to meet in. The Governor vetoed the act, on the ground that the Legislature had no right to remove the seat of Government. The Legislature passed the act over his veto, and in accordance with it assembled at Shawnee Mission, to which place the Governor followed them. But when they presented to him the bills which they had passed, for his signature, he declined to receive the bills, or to recognize them as a lawful Legislature, not because they had not been duly elected, but for the reason that they were assembled in a place not authorized by law. From this time all official relations ceased between the Governor and the Legislature. The Legislature proceeded to pass a full code of laws for the Territory, and as a matter of form presented them to the Governor for his signature, and when he failed to return them, within the time prescribed in the organic act, they reënacted them and declared them to be in force without his signature. Having concluded their legislative duties they adjourned, and about that time President Pierce removed Governor Reeder, for the alleged reason that he had been improperly speculating in Indian lands; and Governor Reeder immediately denounced the acts of the Legislature as being void, for the reason that they had all been elected by fraud, and therefore never constituted a Legislature; that is, *he changed his ground, left the Democratic party, and joined the Republicans or Freesoilers.*

Immediately after the adjournment of the Legislature, the Freesoil party called a Convention, at which they resolved not to recognize or obey the laws which had been passed by the Legislature, nor the authority of the Territorial Government established by Congress, and they provided for calling a Constitutional Convention to frame a Constitution for admission into the Union as a State. Delegates were elected, and the Convention assembled at Topeka in October of that year, 1856, and framed a Constitution, which was submitted to the people for ratification at an election which the Convention ordered to be held under such regulations as should be prescribed by an *executive committee,* of which James H. Lane was chairman, and to whom the returns were to be made and certified. As no one voted at this election, except those who denied the authority of the Territorial Government, the Constitution was, of course, ratified. At the election for delegates to Congress, which was held about the same time, under the authority of a law passed by the Legislature, the Freesoilers refused to vote, alleging as a reason, that if they voted at that election they recognized the validity of the Territorial authority, but ordered through their executive committee another election, to be held one week thereafter, at which they elected Mr. Parrott. The others elected Whitfield. The Freesoilers proceeded also to organize their State Government under the Topeka Constitution, by the election of a Governor and State officers, Legislature and judges. The Legislature thus elected assembled and chose Reeder and Lane United States Senators, who came to Washington and brought the Constitution with them, and demanded admission into the Union. I had been confined by serious illness at Terre Haute, Indiana, that session, 1855 and 1856, and until the month of February. I arrived here (Washington) in very feeble health. The President's annual message, and a special message which he sent to Congress in the month of February, 1856, in regard to this Topeka movement, together with all other matters referring to the disturbances in Kansas, were referred to the Committee on Territories, from which, on the 12th of March, I made an elaborate report, in which I gave a full history of those Kansas difficulties, together with an exposition of the principles of the Kansas-Nebraska Act. The result was, that I reported a bill for the admission of Kansas into the Union when she should have the requisite population for a member of Congress, ninety-three thousand four hundred and twenty, and treating the Topeka Constitution as a nullity, being the result of a revolutionary movement, and recognizing the other, the Territorial Legislature, as a lawful body, and refusing to review its legislative proceedings, considering the validity of the Territorial enactments a judicial question, which it was not competent for the legislative department of the Government to decide. In the House of Representatives Whitfield was declared elected, the House taking the same view of the Topeka Constitution as the Senate did.

The Senate, in their anxiety to close the Kansas controversy, at once substituted a bill introduced by Mr. Toombs, of Georgia, for the bill reported by the Committee on Territories. I acquiesced, and we passed Mr. Toombs' bill by a strict party vote. The bill provided that the people of Kansas might at once proceed to elect delegates to a Convention to frame a State Constitution, in the manner prescribed in the bill, and should be received into the Union on an equal footing with the original States, without regard to the number of their population. The Toombs bill was sent to the House, where all after the enacting clause was stricken out, by a strict party vote, the Republicans having a majority in that House, and a bill for the admission of Kansas into the Union, under the Topeka Constitution, was substituted, and sent to the Senate for concurrence. The Senate disagreed to the amendment of the House, and the bill was lost by the disagreement of the two Houses. *It was evident during all the proceedings that the Republicans were as anxious to keep the Kansas question open as the Democrats were to close it, in view of the approaching Presidential election.*

The Kansas question became the all-absorbing question in the Presidential election of 1856, and came near defeating the election of Mr. Buchanan. When the result of the Presidential election was known, the public mind settled down into the general belief that he would insure a fair expression of the popular opinion in Kansas, in the settlement of their domestic institutions. During the winter of 1856 and 1857, the Territorial Legislature of Kansas passed an act providing for the election of delegates to a Convention to frame a Constitution preparatory to their admission into the Union. By this act it was provided that there should be a registry made of all the legal voters in each of the counties of the Territory, with a view of insuring a fair election, and of excluding all illegal voters; and that when said registry should be completed, it should be the duty of the Governor to apportion the delegates among the different counties, in proportion to the number of legal voters as shown by the registry.

Soon after his inauguration Mr. Buchanan appointed Robert J. Walker Governor and F. P. Stanton Secretary of the Territory of Kansas. Mr. Stanton repaired to the Territory immediately, and performed the duties of Governor until the arrival of Mr. Walker, who was detained at Washington several weeks. When the registry of legal voters was returned to Mr. Stanton, he made the apportionment in accordance with the returns, although it was subsequently shown that fifteen counties, being nearly one-half of the counties in the Territory, had been omitted in the returns, no votes having been registered in those counties. When Mr. Walker was first appointed Governor he declined to accept the appointment, but was induced to reconsider, at the personal solicitation of Mr. Buchanan, and of other friends, and at last consented to accept it, on the condition that upon the comparison of opinions between himself, the President, and his Cabinet, it should be found that they concurred in the policy that the Constitution to be formed by the convention, which had been provided for, should be submitted to the people for ratification or rejection, at a fair election, to be held in pursuance of law, for that purpose, before it should be sent to Congress for acceptance. Mr. Buchanan and his entire Cabinet agreed to this condition as the line of policy to be pursued by the Federal administration. Governor Walker, while yet at Washington, prepared his inaugural address to the people of Kansas, in which he urged the people of all parties in Kansas to vote for delegates at the election which was about to be held, with the assurance that the convention would assemble only for the purpose of framing a Constitution to be submitted to the people for ratification or rejection, and not for the purpose of adopting a Constitution to be put in force without ratification. In this inaugural address, Governor Walker assured the people of Kansas that in the event that the Constitution should not be submitted to the people for ratification, and should not be ratified by a majority of the legal voters at such election, he would use his best efforts to defeat the admission of Kansas under such Constitution, and that he was authorized to say that the President and every member of his Cabinet endorsed this position. When Governor Walker left Washington *en route* for Kansas, he stopped one day in Chicago to consult with me, as he stated, at the request of the President, and to see whether I would endorse and sanction the line of policy upon which they had agreed in respect to the submission of the Constitution to the people; and in order that I might understand precisely what that position was, Governor Walker read his inaugural address to me, *as slightly modified by interlineations in the handwriting of the President of the United States himself.* I said to Governor Walker that while I did not precisely comprehend what right the President and his Cabinet had to interfere with the convention, by insisting that the Constitution should be submitted to the people, yet as a Senator who would have to vote for or against the admission of Kansas under the Constitution, I had no hesitation in saying that I should require satisfactory evidence that the Constitution *was the act and deed of the people of Kansas, and a faithful embodiment of their will,* and that I should regard a ratification by the people at a fair election held for that purpose as the best evidence of that fact. With this assurance Governor Walker proceeded to Kansas, and published his inaugural address, containing these pledges on behalf of himself and of the President and his Cabinet, *that the Constitution must be submitted to the people before Kansas could be admitted into the Union under it.*

When the fact was made known to Governor Walker that there could not be a fair election of delegates by the whole people of Kansas, for the reason that nearly one-half of the counties had been omitted in the registration of votes, and consequently deprived of the privilege of electing delegates to the convention, he issued an address to the people, in which he acknowledged the great wrong which had been done them in the omission to register all the votes in all the counties, and regretted that he had no power, under the law, to correct the error, and appealed to the people to go to the polls, and vote in those counties where a registry had been made, and to trust to the fair dealing of the convention, with the assurance which had been given by the President and his Cabinet, and which he renewed for himself, that the whole people of Kansas would have an opportunity of voting for or against the Constitution, when it should be submitted to the people for ratification or rejection. Many of the people of Kansas, still being sceptical, and doubting whether such an opportunity would be afforded them, called upon the candidates for delegates to pledge themselves in writing to agree to no Constitution which should not be submitted to the people for ratification. In the county of Douglas, which was the largest in the Territory, such a pledge was prepared, signed, and published by John Calhoun, who was subsequently president of the convention, and by all of his associates on the ticket, and upon that pledge they were elected delegates. It is believed, and I am very certain, that similar pledges were given in several other counties, and during the entire canvass for the election of delegates it was conceded that the convention was merely to frame a Constitution, and submit it to the people for ratification, and *not to put it in operation without ratification.*

During that summer, and before the Lecompton Convention assembled, a convention was held, composed of delegates from *all* the counties in the Territory, to nominate a delegate to Congress, to be supported by the Democratic party at the October election; and with a view of securing the votes of the entire Democratic party, free State men as well as proslavery men, a resolution was adopted by a vote of forty to one, pledging the Democratic party to submit the Constitution, which should be framed by the Lecompton Convention, to the people for ratification or rejection. The Lecompton Convention assembled two or three weeks previous to the Territorial election, which was to be held on the first Monday in October, for the election of a delegate to Congress, and for members of the Territorial Legislature, and after organizing by the election of officers, and the appointment of committees, and reference to them of the various parts of the proposed Constitution, the convention adjourned, or took a recess, until after the October election, for the purpose, as it was subsequently avowed, of ascertaining whether the proslavery party or free State party had a majority in the Territory, so far as that fact could be determined by the results furnished by that election. When it became known that the Freesoil party had carried the election by an overwhelming majority, the convention then determined that they would not submit the Constitution to the people, for fear that it would be rejected if they did so, *and therefore determined to submit only one clause, which recognized and established the institution of slavery in the Territory*, and this clause was submitted in such a form as compelled every man who voted for it or against it, to vote for the whole Constitution at the same time, and in the event his vote was challenged, to take an oath to support that Constitution. By *this trick*, for I can fairly call it so, no man was permitted to vote for or against the slavery clause without voting for the Constitution, *when there were provisions in the Constitution itself, elsewhere, and in other parts, than the slavery clause, recognizing and establishing slavery, so that it would be a slave State, whether the proslavery clause was adopted or rejected.*

When Congress assembled in December, 1857, the President of the United States, in his annual message, recommended to Congress to admit Kansas into the Union under the Lecompton Constitution, without reference to the question whether the proslavery clause should or should not be adopted, *and without submitting the Constitution to the ratification or rejection of the people.*

The moment the Secretary of the Senate had concluded the reading of the message, Mr. Douglas rose, and expressed his dissent from so much of the message as related to the admission of Kansas under the Lecompton Constitution, and on the next day he delivered a speech, in which he gave his reasons for such dissent. He objected to the admission of Kansas, under that Constitution, not because of any particular provisions which it contained, *but because there was no satisfactory evidence that it was the act and deed of the people of Kansas, or that it embodied their will,* but, on the contrary, that there was abundance of evidence which warranted the conclusion, *that at least two-thirds, if not four-fifths of the entire population of Kansas were irreconcilably opposed to it.* He stated that his opinions or action on the admission of Kansas under that Constitution would not be in the slightest degree affected by the vote which was to be had on the 21st of that month, for or against the pro-slavery clause, for the reason that they had a right to be heard in respect to the other provisions of the Constitution, as well as that one. *In other words, he maintained that Congress had no right to force a Territory into the Union as a State, against their wishes, or to force upon them a Constitution or institutions against their wills.*

After the result of the election of the 21st of December, on the adoption of the pro-slavery clause, was made known, Mr. Calhoun, president of the Convention, who was also Surveyor-General for the Territories of Kansas and Nebraska, a Federal officeholder, and therefore under the influence of Mr. Buchanan, holding office by his appointment, instead of complying with the directions of the Lecompton Convention, to transmit the Constitution direct to Congress, took it to the President of the United States, who himself transmitted it to Congress, accompanied by a special message, in which he gave his reasons for the admission of Kansas into the Union under it. It was in this message that Mr. Buchanan declared, that it had been decided by the highest judicial tribunal in the land, "*that slavery exists in Kansas by virtue of the Constitution of the United States*," and therefore that Kansas was at that moment as much a slave State as Georgia or South Carolina, and that there was no possible mode in which slavery could be abolished therein, or excluded therefrom, but by the admission of Kansas into the Union as a State.

The Senate passed the bill for the admission of Kansas under the Lecompton Constitution, which was amended in the House of Representatives, by striking out all after the enacting clause, and substituting another bill, which is known as the Crittenden-Montgomery amendment, in consequence of its having been offered by Mr. Crittenden in the Senate, where it was rejected, and renewed in the House by Mr. Montgomery, of Pennsylvania. The Senate refused to agree to the amendment of the House, and after much contention between the two Houses, a Committee of Conference was appointed, composed of three members from each House, who prepared and reported to their respective Houses a substitute for the entire bill, which is known as the English amendment, and which was concurred in by the two Houses, and became the law of the land.

This bill, as it passed, provided in substance that an election should be held in Kansas, for or against the acceptance of certain land grants which were made in the bill to the proposed State of Kansas, for the purposes of education and internal improvements; and if at such election a majority of the votes cast should be in favor of the acceptance of said land grants, such vote should be deemed a ratification of the Lecompton Constitution, and evidence a desire to come into the Union under it; but that, in the event a majority of the votes at that election should be cast against the land grants, the people of Kansas should remain in a territorial condition until the Territory should contain ninety-three thousand four hundred and twenty inhabitants. At the election provided for in the bill, the people rejected the land grants by a majority of *eight to one*, and consequently rejected the Lecompton Constitution, *and thus it died*.

The Montgomery amendment provided, in substance, that the Lecompton Constitution should be submitted to the legal voters of Kansas for ratification or rejection, at a fair election to be held for that purpose, and if at such election a majority of the votes should be cast in favor of this measure, the President of the United States should issue his proclamation declaring Kansas a State of the Union, on an equal footing with the original States; but if a majority of the votes at such election should be cast against the measure, then the people of Kansas were at liberty to proceed to call another Convention, and frame a new Constitution, with which, when submitted to and ratified by the people, Kansas should be admitted into the Union. The chief difference between this measure and the English bill, consisted in the fact, that under the Crittenden amendment, if Kansas rejected the Lecompton Constitution, she could proceed at once to make a new one, and come into the Union with the same population; but by the English bill, if Kansas accepted the Lecompton Constitution, she could come into the Union with thirty-five thousand people, but if she rejected it, she must stay out until she had ninety-three thousand four hundred and twenty. The adoption of the Crittenden-Montgomery amendment, and the refusal to pass the Senate bill for the admission of Kansas under the Lecompton Constitution, was a defeat of the administration, for they staked every thing upon the admission of Kansas under the Lecompton Constitution, without sending it back to the people for ratification or rejection. When defeated in this attempt, they took shelter under the English bill, by submitting the question to the people of Kansas *in an indirect and unfair manner*, but still in such a manner as enabled the people of Kansas to reject it, by voting against the land grants, *which they ardently desired*, and which were a *bribe* to have them vote for it, accompanied with a *penalty, if they did not*, of being obliged to remain out of the Union until they had ninety-three thousand four hundred and twenty inhabitants. Here was *a bribe* and a *threat*. The rejection of the English bill by the people of Kansas rendered the defeat of the administration *complete in all respects*, and was equivalent to an unconditional rejection of the Lecompton Constitution by the Congress at first, with the exception that they gained the provision of the English bill, *forcing Kansas to remain out of the Union until it should have a largely increased population.*

I supported the Crittenden-Montgomery amendment, which would have carried out fully all my wishes and principles, but I opposed violently the English bill.

Question.—In 1852 both Whigs and Democrats endorsed the compromise measures. What became of the Whig party after the defeat of Scott, and what was the origin of the Republican and Know-Nothing parties?

Answer.—The Whigs were so badly beaten, having carried only four States, that they were utterly dispirited, and very unwisely broke up their party organization and disbanded. Soon after, in 1854, the Kansas-Nebraska Bill came before the country, and there arose an anti-Nebraska party, into which most of the Whigs went. This party kept the name Anti-Nebraska for more than a year and a half, and, in 1856, took the name of the Republican party.

In the spring of 1854, pending the Nebraska Bill, the Know-Nothing party arose silently and secretly. The first that was known of it was, when in parts of Pennsylvania, Philadelphia, New Orleans, and other places, persons were elected to office who were not in nomination, and not known to be running till after elected, and when in Washington people were driven from the polls. This party gave vitality and strength to the Republican party. Nearly all the Republicans throughout the country went into its lodges; and a member from Tennessee, by some means, got hold of the names of the Republican members of Congress who were members, and made a speech in the House, in which he called them by name and defied them to deny it. The party struck terror everywhere among the Democrats, and threatened to gain absolute possession of the Government. I tried to get the Democrats in caucus to denounce it, but they refused, and were afraid. General Cass said to me that I had enough to contend with, and could not carry on my shoulders opposition to this new element. I was the first Democrat to make a speech against it. I did so at Independence Hall, Philadelphia. The party received the name Know-Nothing, because its members were instructed to answer "I know nothing" to all questions put to them. It had not principles to make a party—no great issues. It first split between the North and South Americans on the slavery question, and it finally died quickly, being nothing more nor less than the present Republican party merged into it.

I refer you to my speeches in the Senate for the whole argument on the Kansas-Nebraska Act. I passed the Kansas-Nebraska Act myself. I had the authority and power of a dictator throughout the whole controversy in both houses. The speeches were nothing. It was the marshalling and directing of men, and guarding from attacks, and with a ceaseless vigilance preventing surprise.

In opposition, Seward's and Sumner's speeches were mere essays against slavery. Chase, of Ohio, was the leader. Bell *never* made a speech that was an argument.

POPULAR AND SQUATTER SOVEREIGNTY DEFINED AND DISTINGUISHED.

The name of Squatter Sovereignty was first applied by Mr. Calhoun, in a debate in the United States Senate in 1848, between himself and General Cass, in respect to the right of the people of California to institute a government for themselves after the Mexican jurisdiction had been withdrawn from them, and before the laws of the United States had been extended over them. General Cass contended that in such a case the people had a right, an inherent and inalienable right, to institute a government for themselves and for their own protection. Mr. Calhoun replied, that with the exception of the native Californians, the inhabitants of that country were mere squatters upon the public domain, who had gone there in vast crowds, without the authority of law, and were in fact trespassers as well as squatters upon the public lands, and to recognize their right to set up a government for themselves was to assert the doctrine of *Squatter Sovereignty*. The term had no application to an organized Territory under the authority of Congress, or to the powers of such organized Territory, but was applied solely to an unorganized country whose existence was not recognized by law. On the other hand, what is called *Popular Sovereignty* in the Territories, is a phrase used to designate the right of the people of an organized Territory, under the Constitution and laws of the United States, to govern themselves in respect to their own internal polity and domestic affairs.

ORIGIN, HISTORY, AND STATE OF PARTIES, OF MEN AND OF MEASURES,

FROM THE FORMATION OF THE GOVERNMENT DOWN TO THE ADMINISTRATION OF PRESIDENT PIERCE.

UNMISTAKABLE indications were given, in the convention which framed the Federal Constitution, of radical differences of opinion in respect to the character of the Federal Government which they were about to form, and which subsequently, to some extent, entered into the formation of political parties.

There were two parties in the convention arrayed upon the same question, whether a national Government should first be established for the United States, or whether the system of confederated and sovereign States should be continued, with such modifications as experience had proven to be necessary.

Alexander Hamilton was the leader of the extreme national party, who wished to establish a strong national Government, and proposed to elect a President for life; Senators for life; members of the House for a long term of years; the Governors of the States to be appointed by the President of the United States, and all legislative enactments by the States to be subject to the approval or disapproval of the United States. Mr. Madison and Mr. Randolph, of Virginia, while they did not go to the full length of Mr. Hamilton's views, leaned strongly in that direction; while Mr. George Mason, of Virginia, the Rutledges of Carolina, and others, were content with the Articles of Confederation, with slight modifications. Jealousies also arose between the large States and the small ones; the former contending for a voice in the Federal Government in proportion to population, while the latter insisted that each State, being a sovereign power, should have an equal voice in the Federal Government, without reference to population. These conflicting interests prevented either party from carrying out its entire plan, and coerced a compromise, in which all yielded more or less of their opinions. The result was the present Constitution. General Washington was neutral, though leaning to the strong Government, the Federal side.

After the Federal Government was organized, the school of politicians of which Colonel Hamilton was the head, endeavored to make the present Constitution, *by construction*, mean what they would have made it, if they had wielded the power in the convention, while the extreme State Rights men endeavored to curtail the powers of the Federal Government by the opposite rules of construction; while others, of which Mr. Madison was the most distinguished, endeavored to give the Government a fair trial under the Constitution as it had been made and adopted.

The first question of any considerable importance which brought these two systems into conflict, was the charter of the Bank of the United States in 1791; Colonel Hamilton and his school contending that Congress had the power to charter such a bank, while the State Rights school, of which Mr. Jefferson had become the leader, denied the existence of such power in Congress, for the reason that it was not delegated in the Constitution. Mr. Madison took sides with Mr. Jefferson and his friends upon this question.

The next question, which was the most extreme and significant of all, was the enactment of what is popularly known as the Alien and Sedition Laws of 1798. These were two distinct enactments, although usually referred to as one, because involving similar principles. The *Alien Law*, as it is called, authorized the President of the United States to cause any alien who should be found within our limits, and whose presence the President should believe was dangerous to the peace and good order of the country, to be arrested and removed beyond the limits of the United States. The *Sedition Law* made it a criminal offence, punishable with imprisonment, for any person to speak or write injuriously to the reputation of the President, his Cabinet, or any officer of the Government. Under the Sedition Law a large number of Republican or Democratic editors, who were opposed to the Federal administration of John Adams, were arrested and consigned to prison; and one of these from the State of Vermont, while in prison, was elected to Congress.

The Republican party, of which Mr. Jefferson was the acknowledged head, denounced the Alien and Sedition Laws as direct and palpable infractions of the Constitution, and dangerous to the rights and liberties of the people. The power of the Federal Government was at this time so firmly established, that the Republican members of Congress despaired of their ability to render any further service in the national councils; and accordingly Mr. Madison, Mr. Albert Gallatin, and others, retired from Congress, and took seats in their respective State Legislatures, with the hope of organizing State resistance to Federal encroachments. Mr. Jefferson wrote the Kentucky Resolutions of 1798, and forwarded them to his friend, George Nichols, in Kentucky, to be adopted by the Legislature of that State. These resolutions denounced the Alien and Sedition Laws as a violation of the Constitution of the United States, and asserted the doctrine that the Constitution, being a compact between sovereign and independent States, each member of the confederacy had a right to judge for itself of the nature of the compact, and the extent of its violation.

Mr. Madison is understood to be the author of the Resolutions of 1799, adopted by the Virginia Legistature, and was chairman of the committee, and the author of their report enforcing and expounding the doctrines of the Kentucky Resolutions of 1798, and the Virginia Resolutions of 1799.

The Federal party, on the other hand, insisted that each department of the Federal Government was the judge of the extent of its own authority under the Constitution, and that Congress, like the British Parliament, had the exclusive power of determining the extent of their authority, and consequently that the Alien and Sedition Laws must be regarded and held as constitutional, for the reason that Congress had so decided by the act of passing them.

Before the Federal Government and the States were brought into actual collision upon the issues thus presented, the Presidential election of 1800 put an end to the controversy, by the triumph of the Republican party, in the election of Mr. Jefferson, and the consequent rejection of Mr. Adams and his policy. I may here remark, that though Chief-Justice Marshall became the leading intellect of the Federalist party during Mr. Adams's administration, he was constantly charged with being imbued with *Virginia abstractions*, and not to be relied upon in carrying out Federal measures. His integrity and judgment were not doubted.

After the election of 1800, the Federal party dwindled into a small minority, composed in great part of men of large wealth and respectability of character and talents. Mr. Jefferson maintained a majority in both houses of Congress, and was re-elected in 1804 by a very large majority, and held control of all the departments of the Government for the period of eight years, when he was succeeded by Mr. Madison, who had been his Secretary of State during both his terms, and was deemed a faithful exponent of the Jeffersonian policy. Towards the latter part of Mr. Jefferson's administration, questions affecting our maritime rights became serious matters of dispute with Great Britain; such as the right of search exercised by British vessels over American vessels upon the high seas, and the impressment into the British service of all sailors of British birth who were found upon American vessels. In retaliation for these acts, Mr. Jefferson and Mr. Madison recommended embargo laws and non-intercourse laws, which only aggravated the irritation, until it resulted in declaration of war in 1812. Mr. Madison was reëlected, and administered the Government until the 4th of March, 1817, when he was succeeded by Mr. Monroe, who had been a member of his Cabinet, and who was regarded as the legitimate political successor of Madison and Jefferson. During the war a large number of the old Federalist party, including John Quincy Adams, became identified with the Republicans, which fact, to a certain extent, obliterated party lines, although the great body of the Federal party, especially the New England States, took part against the war, and *even sympathized* with the British. Towards the close of the war the leaders of the Federal party in New England held a Convention at Hartford, Connecticut, at which they deliberated, with closed doors, and in secret council, upon the condition of the country, and upon the propriety of forming an alliance with Great Britain, and of withdrawing from the Federal Union. The sudden arrival of the news of peace, however, terminated the war, in a blaze of glory, at New Orleans, and thus put an end to the treasonable schemes of the New England Federalists. The odium attached to the Federal party, and even to the name of Federalist, was so great after the war had closed, that all the politicians in that party who cherished a desire for political promotion, either disavowed the name and joined the Republicans, or proclaimed a truce and sought for new issues upon which new parties could be constructed.

The Bank of the United States having been rechartered in 1816, by the coöperation of the Republican party with its Federal supporters, was for a time taken out of the political issues of the day; and the pecuniary embarrassments and financial derangements consequent upon the war, created a necessity, as was supposed, for increasing duties upon the importation of foreign goods, with discriminations for the encouragement of domestic manufactures. In this measure a large body of the Republicans, with Mr. Calhoun and Cheves, of South Carolina, Lowndes, and other distinguished Southern Republicans, took the lead, as they also did with the re-charter of the Bank of the United States, and in planning and executing a general system of roads, canals, and other internal improvements by the Federal Government. The coöperation of so many Republicans with the great body of the Federalists, upon these several measures, had the effect of almost obliterating party lines, and of producing what was known in the political circles of that day as the *era of good feeling* under Jimmy Monroe's administration. This general harmony, however, was suddenly and fearfully disturbed in 1819, 1820, and 1821, by the introduction of the slavery question as an element of party strife, when the people of Missouri applied to Congress for permission to form a Constitution and State Government preparatory to their admission into the Union. The Northern Federalists sprung upon the country the proposition to prohibit slavery in all the Territories and "new States" hereafter to be organized and admitted into the Union.

It had been the uniform custom of the Republican or Democratic party, from the period of its first organization until 1824, to have the Republican Democratic members of the two houses of Congress assemble in caucus near the expiration of each Presidential term, and nominate candidates for President and Vice-President of the United States, to be supported by the party. As the time approached, towards the close of Mr. Monroe's second term, for the Congressional caucus to assemble and nominate candidates for the succession, jealousies and rivalries arose in the Republican ranks, which divided the party into several factions, each rallying around its favorite leader. Mr. John Quincy Adams, who had become a professed Republican, and was Secretary of State under Mr. Monroe, became a candidate for the Presidency. Mr. William H. Crawford, who was Secretary of the Treasury under Mr. Monroe, also became a candidate. John C. Calhoun, who was Mr. Monroe's Secretary of War, likewise became a candidate. Henry Clay, who was Speaker of the House of Representatives, and had acquired great reputation during the war as a popular leader, became a candidate; while the friends of General Andrew Jackson, who had acquired great glory and renown by his Indian campaigns, and especially by the battle of New

Orleans, presented his name for the Presidency. While these several gentlemen were recognized as candidates by the country, and were supported by their friends as Republicans, and each, in the opinion of their friends, was pronounced the true representative of the Republican party; a small portion of the members of Congress, who still had a great reverence for the usages of the party, assembled in caucus, and nominated William H. Crawford, of Georgia, for President, and Martin Van Buren, of New York, for Vice-President, and declared them to be the regularly nominated candidates, according to the usages of the party. The friends of Adams, Clay, Calhoun, and General Jackson, all refused to recognize the binding force of the nominations made by the Congressional caucus, and appealed to the country to support their respective favorites. Before the time of election however arrived, the friends of Mr. Calhoun, in Pennsylvania, in which State he expected the largest support, because of his high tariff and internal improvement doctrines, withdrew his name, and united upon General Jackson as their candidate, and presented the name of Mr. Calhoun for Vice-President, in which movement Calhoun acquiesced. When the result of the election was known, it appeared that General Jackson had received the highest number of electoral votes, that Mr. Adams stood next highest on the list, Mr. Crawford third, and Mr. Clay fourth, and that no one having received a majority, the election was referred to the House of Representatives, where, according to the provisions of the Constitution, the choice was confined to the three highest; consequently Mr. Clay was ruled out as being ineligible, by the House, where it was supposed that, in consequence of his personal popularity with the members, he would have been chosen, if eligible. Under these circumstances, it was conceded on all hands that Mr. Clay held the balance of power, and could give the Presidency to whichever of the three he preferred. The extreme ill health and protracted sickness of Mr. Crawford put him out of the question, and reduced the contest to the choice of either Jackson or Adams. Great doubts were for a long time entertained which Mr. Clay would choose, there not being cordial relations between himself and General Jackson, and a deadly hostility, involving an *adjourned question of veracity*, existing between himself and Mr. Adams, whose conduct at the Treaty of Ghent he had fiercely denounced, charging him with having proposed to sell out the free navigation of the Mississippi River, out of hostility to the West, for an interest in the Eastern cod-fisheries. It was charged at the time, and the name of James Buchanan, of Pennsylvania, given as the author, that Mr. Clay sent a message to General Jackson, that he would make him President, provided General Jackson would appoint him Secretary of State, and that General Jackson indignantly rejected the proposition, declaring that his right hand should never know what his left would do. Immediately afterwards the friends of Mr. Clay voted for Mr. Adams, and secured his election, and Mr. Adams appointed Mr. Clay Secretary of State. The whole land was filled at once with charges of bargain and corruption between Mr. Adams and Mr. Clay, and a coalition was formed between the friends of Jackson, Crawford, and Calhoun, to oppose and break down the administration, and in 1828 all the opposition united upon General Jackson for President and Calhoun for Vice-President, and secured their election by an overwhelming majority. From the election of General Jackson dates the reconstruction of the old Republican party, under the name of the Democratic party, which has ever since continued with its organization intact, although it has modified its position upon some of the questions upon which it was founded, while many others have in the progress of events become obsolete.

Immediately after the inauguration of General Jackson, a violent opposition was organized by Mr. Calhoun and his Southern associates, against the protective tariff which had been adopted in 1828, and which soon gave indications of a settled purpose to resist the collection of the revenue under the laws of Congress, by interposing State authority, claiming for its sanction the resolutions of 1798 and 1799. This doctrine was for the first time formally proclaimed and avowed in the Senate in 1830, in the famous debate between Hayne and Webster. The Legislature of South Carolina, under the advice of Mr. Calhoun, passed an act calling a Convention of delegates to be elected by the people of the State, to assemble, and by virtue of their sovereign power, as a member of the Confederacy, to annul the act of Congress, the tariff act, by pronouncing it null and void, and declaring that it should never be executed within the limits of that State. Mr. Hayne, the leader of the nullifiers in the Senate, resigned his seat in that body, and accepted the office of Governor of South Carolina, for the purpose of conducting in person State resistance to Federal authority, and Mr. Calhoun resigned his office of Vice-President of the United States, and accepted a seat in the Senate to fill Mr. Hayne's vacancy, as the champion of nullification in that body. General Hamilton, of South Carolina, was appointed by Governor Hayne commander-in-chief of the military forces of the State, and in order to produce a collision with the Federal authorities, purchased a vessel and sent it to Cuba to be laden with sugar and return to Charleston without paying duties. In view of these facts, President Jackson issued a proclamation, warning the people of South Carolina of the perilous consequences of resisting the laws of the United States, and appealing to their patriotism to return to their allegiance, and avowing his fixed purpose to enforce the laws of the United States, and to reduce all rebels to subjection by the use of the whole power of the country if necessary. He also sent a special message to Congress, communicating all the facts, and asking for additional powers and authority to enable him to enforce the laws; and he did not hesitate on all occasions to avow his purpose to seize and hang Mr. Calhoun the first instant that blood was shed. At this stage of the proceedings Mr. Clay introduced into the Senate a bill for the modification of the tariff, which is usually known as Clay's Compromise Tariff Bill, by the provisions of which the tariff duties were to be reduced by a regular ratio each year for ten years, when the highest rate of duty should be fixed at 20 per cent. *ad valorem.* Mr. Calhoun accepted this bill as a compromise, and it passed both houses of Congress and became the law of the land. Thus ended nullification.

When the tariff duties, in 1842, reached the standard of twenty per cent. *ad valorem* by gradual reductions, the Whig party, then being in power, passed a new protective tariff bill, known, according to the party slang of that day, as the Black Tariff, which imposed higher protective duties, and was consequently more obnoxious to the free-traders of the South, than even the tariff of 1828. This tariff bill continued in force until 1846, when the Democrats, having succeeded to power under Mr. Polk, repealed it, and substituted in its place the revenue tariff of 1846, which continued in force until 1856, when, in consequence of the large surplus revenue received under it, it was modified, with the view of reducing the revenue, without materially changing its principles. The Whigs held to the protective principle, and the Democrats the revenue principle.

The following is the origin of the name of the Whig party:

After General Jackson had vetoed the United States Bank in July, 1832, and removed the public deposits from the Bank of the United States in September, 1833, he was denounced by all the friends of the bank and the opponents of his administration as a tyrant, who carried out his own prejudices and purposes regardless of law, and in violation of the Constitution. The Senate of the United States then consisted of a majority opposed to his administration, in consequence of the coalition between Mr. Calhoun and his followers, and the opposition party, headed by Clay and Webster, and which, from the time of General Jackson's election to the Presidency, had been known as the National Republican party. At this period James Watson Webb, editor of the New York "Courier and Enquirer," had received a loan from the Bank of the United States of $52,000, and on the next day his paper denounced General Jackson and his administration, which he had previously supported, for vetoing the bank, and increased its denunciations when he removed the deposits, and appealed to all the opposition to General Jackson by whatever name they had been previously known, or whatever might have been their past affinities, to unite in rescuing the Government from the hands of the tyrant, *under the name of* Whig. He went into a history of the Whig party of England to show that it was an honored and revered name, and that its chief characteristic was opposition to the prerogatives, usurpations, and tyrannies of the crown, asserting that such a party was then needed in this country to maintain the same position, and sustain the same principles; and that for this reason he should hereafter call the opposition by the name of the *Whig* party. The opposition papers throughout the country generally copied General Webb's article and adopted the name, and in the course of a few months the party was known all over the Union as the Whig party. But while the name was changed from National Republican to Whig, the principles of the party remained the same. They continued to be the advocates of the Bank of the United States, of a protective tariff, and of a system of internal improvements by the Federal Government—these being its chief measures.

The quarrel between Mr. Calhoun and General Jackson, early in his administration, led to a dissolution of General Jackson's Cabinet, in consequence of one portion of it being devoted to the political fortunes of Mr. Calhoun. Martin Van Buren, the Secretary of State, who was General Jackson's especial friend, set the example to all the other members of the Cabinet by tendering his resignation, upon the ground that no administration could be successful without *unity in the Cabinet.* The other members all followed Mr. Van Buren's example, and General Jackson accepted the resignations of all the Cabinet, and, at the same time, recalled Louis McLane, of Delaware, who was minister to England, to accept a seat in his new Cabinet, and appointed Mr. Van Buren his successor at the Court of St. James. When the Senate assembled, Mr. Calhoun and his friends made a coalition with the National Republican party, headed by Clay and Webster, to reject the nomination of Mr. Van Buren as minister to England, upon the alleged ground that he had referred in an improper manner to our domestic party questions in an official despatch to the British Government, but on the real ground, as the country believed, of themselves striking a mortal blow at the success of General Jackson's administration. This attempt gave rise to a bitter and exciting debate in the Senate, in secret executive session, which was subsequently published. When the vote was taken the Senate was evenly divided, and consequently it devolved upon Mr. Calhoun, the Vice-President, to give the casting vote, which he did, against the confirmation of Mr. Van Buren. The moment this result was announced, the Democratic party throughout the country, and especially the friends of Mr. Van Buren, raised the cry of persecution, and immediately placed his name at the head of their papers for Vice-President of the United States in place of Mr. Calhoun, to preside over the same body which had rejected his nomination to England. A National Convention was held at Baltimore in 1832, by which General Jackson was nominated for the Presidency, and Mr. Van Buren for the Vice-Presidency, by a unanimous vote, General Jackson having no competitors, and all the previous candidates for the Vice-Presidency withdrawing in favor of Mr. Van Buren. He was elected Vice-President at the same time that General Jackson was reëlected President, and on the 4th of March, 1833, he took his seat as the presiding officer of the Senate, Calhoun, Webster, and Clay, who had been the chief instruments of his rejection, being then all members of that body. The sympathy and enthusiasm created for Mr. Van Buren by his rejection as minister to England, and the favor extended to him by General Jackson, indicated him as General Jackson's successor so plainly, that all competitors deemed it useless to contest his nomination; and all of the leading Democrats, who were unwilling to support the election of Mr. Van Buren, had no other alternative than to take refuge in the ranks of the opposition under the lead of Clay, Webster, and Calhoun. Mr. Van Buren was nominated at Baltimore in 1835, without opposition, as the Democratic candidate for the Presidency, and, in November, 1836, was elected President by an overwhelming majority, the opposition to him in the Northern States voting for William Henry Harrison, and in the Southern, for Hugh S. White, of Tennessee.

Within a few weeks after the inauguration of Mr. Van Buren, on the 4th of March, 1837, the pecuniary revulsion took place which caused all the banks in the country to suspend specie payments, and brought bankruptcy upon the Federal Treasury, being deprived of its revenues and the means of paying its debts and daily expenses, by the failure of the banks, with which the public revenues were deposited. Mr. Van Buren was reduced to the necessity of convening an extra session of Congress, which assembled early in September of that year, and to which, in his annual message, he recommended his famous Sub-Treasury measure, for the divorce of the Government from all banking institutions, and the collection of all the public revenues in gold and silver to be deposited in and paid out directly from the Federal Treasury.

To the astonishment of all his political associates and allies, as well as of his adversaries, Mr. Calhoun gave his efficient and ardent support to the Sub-Treasury measure, and immediately became reconciled to Mr. Van Buren, and the ardent supporter of his administration. The Sub-Treasury was adopted by the two Houses of Congress, and became the law of the land. But the pecuniary revulsion was so great, and the distress of the community so overwhelming, that the people of the country could not be made to believe that the Democratic party, and the Federal administration under General Jackson and Mr. Van Buren, were not in a great measure responsible for the evils under which they labored. The Whig party assembled in National Convention at Harrisburg, Pa., on the 1st of December, 1839, and nominated General W. H. Harrison, of Ohio, for President, and John Tyler, of Virginia, for Vice-President; and refrained from laying down any platform of principles, leaving the candidates entirely uncommitted on every measure of public policy, and the party entirely free in each locality to appeal to the peculiar local prejudice, and to represent their candidates to be for or against each measure of Government, according as it was popular or unpopular in that particular neighborhood. *The cry of change in the Government was the great rallying point*, and the consequence was that Harrison and Tyler carried a majority in all the States of the Union except six, one Northern and five Southern.

General Harrison died at the end of one month from the day of his inauguration, and Mr. Tyler took the oath and assumed the duties of the office of President. He immediately issued his proclamation for a special session of Congress, and invited the Cabinet of General Harrison all to retain their places as his Cabinet. When Congress assembled Mr. Clay assumed the leadership of the party, and arraigned the Democratic party as responsible for the evils which had befallen the country, and held them up as condemned criminals, with halters around their necks, ready to be led out to execution. His programme of measures for the new administration was the same that he had advocated as a member of Mr. Adams's administration, and as the leader of the National Republican or opposition party under the first term of General Jackson, and of the Whig opposition party during the second term of General Jackson and the one term of Mr. Van Buren's administration, to wit: A National Bank, in the place of the Sub-Treasury; a high protective tariff, in the place of his own compromise tariff of 1832; and a system of internal improvements by the Federal Government. The Sub-Treasury was repealed, and a protective tariff passed. The latter was approved by President Tyler; but when they presented to him the bill chartering the Bank of the United States for his approval, he returned it with a veto message, giving his reasons for not signing it, upon the ground of want of power in Congress to pass the law, and referred to his votes and speeches and reports in Congress, and, in short, to his whole political life, to show that he had always been opposed to a United States Bank, and was irrevocably committed against its constitutionality.

Mr. Clay immediately denounced Mr. Tyler as a traitor to the Whig party and as false to those by whom he had been elected, and called upon the party throughout the country, and in both Houses of Congress, to withdraw their confidence, and to make war upon his administration. The leaders of the Democratic party, while they approved Mr. Tyler's veto of the bank, and sustained him in that one measure, withheld their support and countenance from his administration, and left him without any party to rely upon for support, except five or six members of the House, headed by Henry A. Wise and Caleb Cushing, who were known as the "Corporal's Guard." All of the cabinet resigned instantly, with the exception of the Secretary of State, Mr. Webster, who continued to administer his department. When the annexation of Texas was urged by Mr. Tyler, Mr. Webster resigned, and Mr. Upshur, of Virginia, became Secretary of State; and upon the explosion on board of the steamer Princeton, by which Judge Upshur was killed, Mr. Calhoun was appointed Secretary of State, and negotiated the treaty with Texas for the annexation of that Republic to the United States, which treaty was rejected by the Senate by a union of the leaders of both parties, more in consequence of hostility to Mr. Tyler and Mr. Calhoun, and to deprive them of the credit of the measure, than of any well-founded opposition to the measure itself.

Upon the rejection of this treaty, the young men of the Democratic party, in the House of Representatives, who did not participate in the intensity of the prejudice against Mr. Tyler, took up the measure and passed a joint resolution for the annexation of Texas. Under that form the measure passed both Houses of Congress, and was approved by Mr. Tyler only one or two days previous to the inauguration of President Polk. Texas accepted the propositions contained in the joint resolution for annexation, and in December, 1845, was admitted into the Union on an equal footing with the original States.

The Texas question, thus sprung upon the country by Mr. Tyler's administration, was the controlling element in the Presidential election of 1844. The Whig party assembled in convention at Baltimore early in May of that year, and nominated Henry Clay as their candidate for President. The delegates had already been elected by the conventions in the several States to the Democratic National Convention at Baltimore, in June, 1844, a large majority, and in fact nearly all of them, pledged and instructed to vote for the nomination of Mr. Van Buren, as the Democratic candidate. Mr. Clay and Mr. Van Buren had, for months previous to the assembling of either convention, been universally regarded as the chosen candidates of their respective parties, and no other candidates had been thought of by either party, until Mr. Tyler threw this Texas fire-brand or bomb-shell into their midst. Mr. Clay and Mr. Van Buren each was confident that he could beat the other, on the old issues which divided the two parties, and were alike afraid to take either side of the Texas question, for fear of giving the other the advantage. Mr. Clay had been spending the winter with his friend Dr. Mercer in New Orleans, and in the months of March and April made a tour through the Southern States, on his way to Washington and Baltimore, to attend the Whig National Convention. When he arrived at Raleigh, in North Carolina, he remained a few days, where he was met by Mr. Crittenden and other friends from Washington, who it was understood and believed bore assurances from Silas Wright and Mr. Benton, in behalf of Mr. Van Buren, that if he, Mr. Clay, would take moderate grounds against the annexation of Texas, and especially would ignore it in the approaching Presidential election, he, Mr. Van Buren, in behalf of the Democratic party, and already regarded as virtually the nominee, would do the same thing, and thus the leaders of the two great parties would crush out Tylerism and Calhounism, by ignoring the Texas question, and having a fair fight upon the old issues of their respective parties. Accordingly, Mr. Clay published at Raleigh his celebrated letter upon the annexation of Texas, and a few days afterwards Mr. Van Buren published at Kinderhook a similar letter upon the same question. While Mr. Clay had sufficient control over the Whig party to induce them to accept the issue which he had made, Mr. Van Buren's letter created a general revolt in the Democratic ranks. In Virginia, the State central committee was immediately assembled, and released the delegates from that State from their instructions to support Mr. Van Buren, there not being time to call a State convention for that purpose. The example of Virginia was followed in other States, wherever there was time to act, and public meetings were called throughout the country, denouncing the position of Mr. Van Buren on the Texas question, and demanding the nomination of some new man who was pledged to that measure. New candidates came into the field, springing up on all sides, ready to pledge themselves to the annexation of Texas, and joined in the general cry against Van Buren, each supposing that he would get the nomination, if by their joint efforts they could defeat Van Buren's nomination. When the Democratic National Convention assembled at Baltimore, it was ascertained that there was still a majority of the delegates who considered themselves bound in honor by their instructions to vote for the nomination of Mr. Van Buren, a large number of whom were, however, reluctant to give the vote, from the conviction that his nomination would inevitably result in the defeat of the party. On the other hand, the *peculiar* friends of Mr. Van Buren, who comprised nearly one-half of the delegates, insisted upon his nomination, and declared openly that they preferred defeat with him to success with any other living man. In this state of the case, those who felt bound to vote for Mr. Van Buren's nomination, but who were anxious that he should not be nominated, from the fear that it would result in the defeat of the party, joined with his open enemies in the readoption of an old rule which had prevailed in the previous conventions, requiring two-thirds of all the votes to constitute a nomination, and the two-thirds rule was adopted. Mr. Van Buren received a majority of the votes on several ballots, but less than two-thirds, when his vote became less and less, until he was withdrawn; when his friends, with a view of defeating the nomination of General Cass, who was the strongest candidate against him, and whom they regarded as the chief instrument in organizing the opposition to him, presented the name of James K. Polk, of Tennessee, having a letter already in their possession, committing him to the annexation of Texas. Mr. Polk was nominated by a large majority, by a union of a portion of the friends of Texas with the Van Buren men.

The nomination of Mr. Polk, with his known position in favor of the annexation of Texas, and also in favor of *firm, high ground* against the pretensions of England in the Oregon question, made these two the leading issues in the election, and enabled him to defeat Mr. Clay.

The annexation of Texas during Mr. Polk's administration resulted in the Mexican war, the re-adoption of the Sub-Treasury, and the enactment of a revenue tariff, in place of the protective tariff of 1842. During the war, however, and when he asked for an appropriation of money to enable him to pay the first installment for any territory which he might acquire by a treaty of peace, the Wilmot Proviso, prohibiting slavery in the territory to be acquired, was suddenly sprung upon the House and the country, by the *peculiar* friends of Mr. Van Buren, who had become very hostile to Mr. Polk, in consequence of his appointing Governor Marcy into his Cabinet, as the representative of the anti-Van Buren wing of the party in New York, and now took this course for the purpose of embarrassing him and of crippling his administration.

As the time approached for the assembling of the National Convention at Baltimore, in the spring of 1848, to nominate the Democratic candidates for President and Vice-President, the contest became very fierce in the Democratic party in regard to the Wilmot Proviso; and two sets of delegates made their appearance at Baltimore from the State of New York, each claiming to be the true representatives of the party, the one supporting and the other opposing the proviso. The Convention sympathized with the delegates who were opposed to the Wilmot Proviso, but, under the impression that the others had the regular organization of the party, declined to decide upon their respective claims, and passed a resolution for the admission of both sets of delegates, who should jointly, and in such a manner as they might agree upon among themselves, cast the thirty-six votes for the State of New York. The Wilmot Proviso Van Buren delegates, however, refused to accede to this proposition, and declined to take seats in the Convention, upon the ground that they were the regularly appointed delegates, and had a right to cast the entire vote of the State.

General Cass, of Michigan, was nominated for

President, and William O. Butler, of Kentucky, for Vice-President; and when the Wilmot Proviso delegates returned home to New York, they immediately issued a call for a State Convention of their followers, or wing of the party, to assemble at Herkimer, at which Convention it was resolved to call a Convention of all the opponents to the extension of slavery, at Buffalo, in the month of August of that year. At the Buffalo Convention, composed of delegates from all the free States, Mr. Van Buren was nominated for President, and Charles Francis Adams for Vice-President. The Whigs nominated Taylor and Fillmore, having no platform, and leaving each State Convention to make their own. In consequence of the division of the Democratic party in the State of New York into two equal parts, between Van Buren and Cass, General Taylor received the electoral vote of that State, and was elected President of the United States.

When the division in the New York Democracy arose, they were first called "Hunkers" and "Barnburners." The former were national men, the latter Wilmot Proviso men. Subsequently a compromise was made between the Hunkers and Barnburners, by which the party was reunited, and the electoral vote of the State given to General Pierce in 1852;

but in consequence of the removal of Judge Bronson from the office of Collector of the Port of New York, by Mr. Pierce's administration, the old controversy was reopened, and when the old "Hunkers," under the lead of Daniel S. Dickinson, withdrew from the regular organization, and denounced Mr. Pierce's administration, Governor Marcy, who was Secretary of State under Mr. Pierce, and was the leader of the old "Hunker" party during the Wilmot Proviso controversy under Mr. Polk's administration, together with Governor Seymour and other "Hunkers," remained with the regular organization of the party, and sustained Mr. Pierce. From this time Marcy and his "Hunker" friends, who had become identified with the "Barnburners," were called the "Softs," and Dickinson and his party of bolters assumed the name of the "Hards."

THE TARIFF.

Clay and Webster were leading protective tariff men.

In 1816 or 1817 Webster was the champion of free trade. Commerce was then the leading interest of his constituency. But all this changed, and manufactures began largely to employ the labor and the capital of New England. *Then Webster became a protectionist.* On the other hand, in 1816 and 1817, Calhoun was the champion of *protection;* and when Webster became a protectionist, Calhoun became a *free trader.*

Henry Clay was throughout always a protectionist.

This question of a protective tariff has been argued more upon grounds of its expediency and justice than of its constitutionality. Nobody even argued that the Supreme Court would have declared it unconstitutional. The Court would have said it was a political question, which the Government must determine, and would not have annulled it. It would have said the political department had determined the question, and Government must have the choice of means.

The clause of the Constitution which authorizes Congress "to make all laws which shall be necessary and proper for carrying into execution the foregoing powers," confers no power, but is declaratory of a rule of construction which would have been implied if it had not been specified, and is the best rule of construction. The means must be necessary, but need not be *indispensable*—proper, but not the *only proper ones;* and the discretion in choosing the means, where there are a variety of means, is vested within the scope of the Constitution, in the political department of the Government.

The argument of the Democrats upon the tariff question has been, that the Government is limited to the powers delegated by the Constitution, and that those powers must be executed for the *purposes* of the Constitution; and that while the Government has the right to tax imports for the *purposes of revenue*, it has not for the *purpose of protection.*

The argument on the other side is, that while it imposes taxes on imports for revenue, it may do it in such a manner as to protect domestic manufactures; for example, tax high the foreign *manufactured* article, and admit free, or with a small tax, the *materials* of which that article is composed, so as to be manufactured in this country. The Democrats say this is an *abuse of the power*. The present tariff is, however, incidentally protective. The tariff question has ceased to be a political issue, there being men in both parties, and in all parts of the country, who take different views and stand upon both sides.

THE PUBLIC LAND SYSTEM OF THE UNITED STATES.

The foundation of the present system was laid about the time the Constitution was adopted. It consists of a system of surveys, by which the public lands are first laid out into townships, six miles square; each township is subdivided into sections of one mile square, so that there are thirty-six sections in a township; each section is subdivided into four quarters, each one-half mile square; each quarter section is divided into two eighty acre tracts, which are called half quarters, and are designated respectively as the east and west half of the northeast, northwest, southeast, or southwest quarter, and each eighty acre tract is again divided into two forty acre tracts. The following figure will illustrate:

In this figure, A B represents the base line, and C D the meridian. The meridians are all numbered. The one chosen for illustration is in Illinois, and is the third principal meridian.

The figure represents a district of country divided into townships. A township must lie north or south

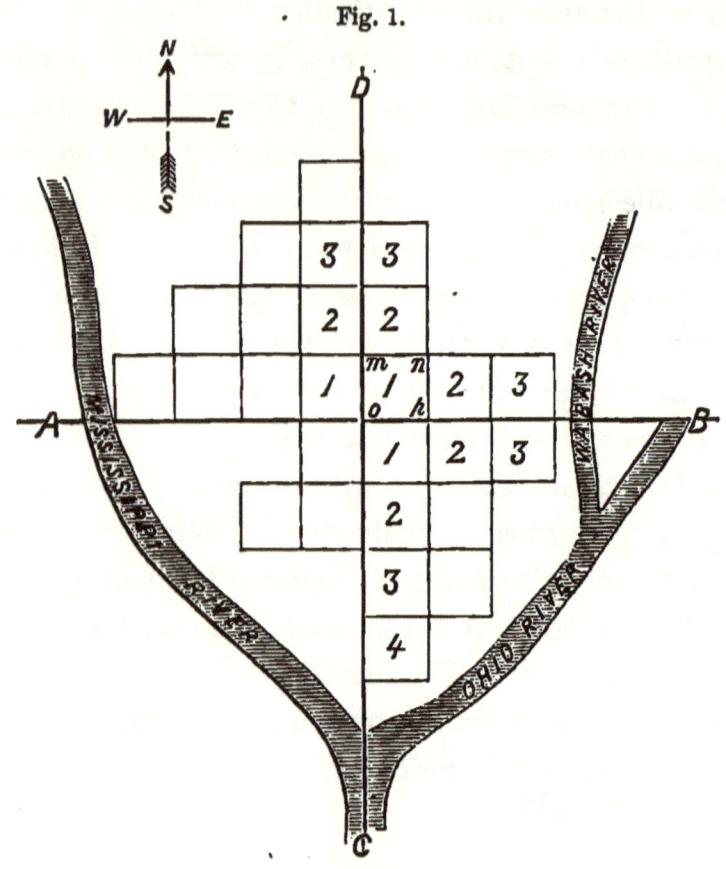

Fig. 1.

of the base line A B, and east or west of the meridian (third principal) C D.

O. M. N. P. would therefore be described as township 1, north 1, east 1, of the third principal meridian; or, T. 1, N. 1, E. 1, 3 P. M.

THE PUBLIC LAND SYSTEM. 163

Figure 2 represents a township divided into sections. They commence by numbering the sections at the northeast corner of each township. Sup-

Fig. 2.

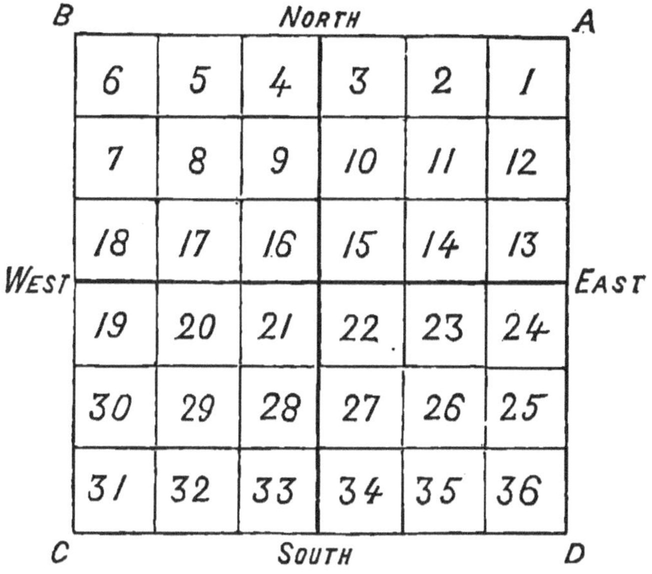

	B	NORTH				A	
	6	5	4	3	2	1	
	7	8	9	10	11	12	
WEST	18	17	16	15	14	13	EAST
	19	20	21	22	23	24	
	30	29	28	27	26	25	
	31	32	33	34	35	36	
	C	SOUTH				D	

pose this figure to represent township I, N. 1, E. 1, 3 P. M., and that we wish to describe section thirty-five. It would be section thirty-five, township 1, north 1, east 1, 3 P. M.

Formerly only one section in each township was given for school purposes, and this was section sixteen. Since the admission of Minnesota two sections in each township are given, and these are sections sixteen and thirty-six. I introduced this improvement.

Figure three represents a section subdivided into quarters, which are the N. E., S. E., N. W., and S. W. quarters of the section respectively. Suppose it to represent section one, township one, north one, east one, third principal meridian, and you wish to describe the northeast quarter. It would be N. E. ¼, S. 1, T. 1, N. 1, E. 1, 3 P. M.

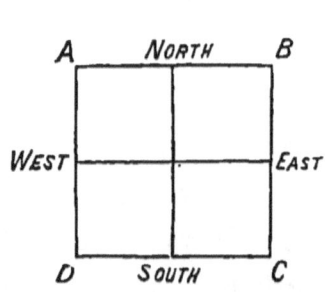

Figure four represents the same northeast quarter of same section, or any other quarter and section divided into eighty acre tracts, which are designated as the east and west half of the northeast quarter, section one, and so on.

Figure five represents the same northeast quarter same section, or any other, divided into forty-eight tracts, or quarters of a quarter, and would be described as the N. E. ¼ of the N. E. ¼, and so on.

This is the perfected system.

The first step is the extinguishment of the Indian title by a treaty with the Indian tribe owning the possessory right, and which, like all other treaties, must be ratified by two-thirds of the Senate. The next step is the survey of the land according to the system above described.

According to the existing laws, there is a *preemption* right given to the settlers upon the lands. By the preëmption law of 1841, and its subsequent amendments, a person may go and settle upon any lands to which the Indian title has been extinguished, erect his house, enclose a portion of the land, and cultivate the same. By making proof of these facts, *residence, cultivation,* and *enclosure,* before the land officers of the proper district, *prior to the day of sale,* the preëmptor becomes entitled to buy the tract upon which he resides, and upon which his improvements are located, not exceeding one quarter section, or one hundred and sixty acres, at one dollar and twenty-five cents per acre, which is the minimum price at which the lands are sold.

After the surveys are completed, Congress provides by law that all the lands situated within the following limits, describing them, shall constitute a land district, by the following name or number, designating the district, and that there shall be a land office established therein, for the sale of the public lands within said district, and that the President shall appoint, by and with the advice and consent of the Senate, a Register and Receiver for said land office. It is the duty of the Register to keep the records and plans of survey of all the lands within the district, and of the Receiver to receive all moneys in payment of lands sold by the Register.

Before any of the lands are allowed to be sold at private sale, the President of the United States issues his proclamation, designating some future day, usually from three to six months distant, at which all or a portion of the lands within said district will be offered at public auction, describing the lands in the proclamation by their numbers, and giving notice that, before the day of sale, all persons claiming preëmption on any of said lands will be required to appear at the land office and make the requisite proofs in support of their claims, and to pay the money for the same, otherwise they will be sold at auction the same as the other lands. When the day of sale arrives, the Register of the land office, with the maps before him, puts up each tract at auction, beginning with the east half of the northeast quarter of section one, in the township, and thus exposing in their order each eighty acre tract or half quarter section to the highest bidder, receiving no bid less than one dollar and a quarter per acre, and striking off the tract to the highest bidders. When the sales of the day shall have closed, a *certificate* is made out to each purchaser, describing the tract purchased by him, by its number and description, according to the system already explained. The purchaser presents this certificate to the Receiver as the evidence that he is entitled to that tract of land upon the payment of the money. The Receiver receives the money, and takes up the certificate, and gives the purchaser a receipt certifying that he has paid the money for the land therein described, and stating the number of acres in the tract, the amount paid, and the rate per acre. This receipt is called a *duplicate*, for the reason that the Receiver makes out two at the same time, the other of which is forwarded to the United States land office at Washington, and upon which a patent issues to the purchaser, over the signature of the President and the seal of the United States, written on parchment, which becomes the title deed of the land.

When any tract of land is thus offered by the Register, and nobody present bids one dollar and a quarter per acre, the tract is struck off to the United States, and the next tract is offered in its order. The sales continue in this manner from day to day, until all the lands specified in the President's proclamation have been offered for sale, when the sale is declared to be closed, and all further business in the office is suspended for a certain number of days, to enable the land officers to make up their records, and transmit their returns of sales in due form to the General Land Office; which being done, the land office, upon proper notice by the Register, is again opened, and all the lands are exposed from that time to *private sale*, with the privilege on the part of any person who wishes to purchase, to do so by applying to the Register for a certificate to the Receiver for any tract or tracts he may select, at one dollar and a quarter per acre, the minimum price fixed; and upon delivering that certificate to the Receiver, and paying his money, he receives his duplicate, as in the case of a sale made at public auction. But in case two or more persons apply to the Register *at the same time*, and for the *same tract of land*, the Register receives bids from each in the *presence of the others*, and issues his certificate to the highest bidder, specifying the rate per acre, the number of acres, and the amount of money to be paid.

Prior to 1820 the public lands were sold on a credit of one, two, three, four, and five years, at two dollars per acre, and that fact gave rise to the provision in the compacts between the United States, and the States of Ohio, Indiana, Illinois, and Louisiana, and in short all the States admitted into the Union previous to 1820, by which each of said States pledged their faith, in consideration of certain grants of land for schools and internal improvements, not to tax the lands of the United States within their respective limits for the period of five years after the date of sale. The object of this stipulation was to prevent any person from obtaining a tax title under the authority of the State, before the United States had received the full amount of the purchase money.

The credit system, for the sale of the public lands, produced the most ruinous consequences in stimulating speculation and inducing people to purchase vast quantities, for which they were not able to make payments in cases of pecuniary revulsions. This was partly the case in 1817-'18, and 1819, when the settlers upon the public lands, and others who were speculating in them, found themselves indebted to the United States for many millions of dollars which they were unable to pay, and being unwilling to forfeit the installments which they had paid, they petitioned Congress for relief, and a compromise, by which they might be permitted to receive a quantity of the land purchased equal to the payments they had made, and be released from the remainder, was asked for. The relief was granted, and the land system was changed so far as to abolish the credit system entirely, and to reduce the price from $2 to $1.25 per acre.

A few years ago Congress passed an act known as the "Graduation Bill," to the effect that all lands which had been offered at public sale, and remained unsold at private sale for the period of ten years, should be reduced in price to one dollar per acre; over ten years and less than fifteen, seventy-five cents; over fifteen and less than twenty, fifty cents; over twenty and less than twenty-five, twenty-five cents; and over twenty-five years, twelve and a half cents per acre, provided that no person was permitted to enter any land at these reduced prices, unless he was an actual settler upon the same, and should make oath that he purchased the same for his own use and cultivation, or that the lands were adjoining the farm upon which he did reside, and that the purchase was made for the purpose of enlarging his farm and for his own use, and not to be transferred to another; and that in no case should any one person purchase more than one quarter section at the reduced prices. Under this law the most shameful abuses were perpetrated by men making false oaths, entering vast tracts of lands, in some instances in the names of their infant children and grandchildren not even three weeks old, oftentimes by connivance of the public officers, and by hiring persons to enter lands in different districts.

By reference to the compacts between the United States and the several new States admitted into the Union, it will be observed that the section numbered sixteen in each township throughout the entire State has been granted for the purpose of public schools; seventy-two sections, equal to two entire townships, for the purpose of establishing a State University, and five per cent. of the gross proceeds of all the sales of the public lands within such State, together with all the salt springs, not exceeding twelve in number, and one section to each, were granted to the State for the purposes of education and internal improvements, which grant was deemed and held to be in consideration of the surrender by such State of any equitable claim it might have to tax the lands and property of the United States within their limits.

Some thirty years ago Congress granted to Ohio, Indiana, and Illinois, the alternate sections for five miles on each side of the lines of certain canals, which said States proposed to make, to aid in their construction. No other reason seems to have actuated or induced the action of Congress in these cases, except to aid those States in the construction of their works. In 1850 a Senator from Illinois introduced a bill granting to that State the alternate sections for six miles on each side of the line of the Illinois Central Railroad and its branches, on condition that the said State should make or cause said railroad to be made, within ten years from the date of the grant, and that the United States mails should be forever transported on the same, under the direction of the Post-office Department, at a fair compensation; and in the event of a disagreement Congress should fix the same; and on the further condition that the other alternate sections should be sold at $2.50 per acre, so as to enable the United States to receive for the reserved half as much as they claimed for the whole, and which thirty years' experience had shown that she could not get for the whole—these lands having been in the market during that period at $1.25 per acre, and remaining unsold. The bill passed, and the State granted the lands to the Illinois Central Railroad Company, on condition that the company would complete the road within six years instead of ten, and forever comply with the terms and conditions of the act of Congress in all respects. The company completed the road in four years, and the United States sold all the lands within a few months at prices ranging from $2.50 to $7.25 per acre. All the grants which have been made to other States for railroads were founded upon the same principles as the Illinois case, *but candor forces the admission that the same results have not been produced in any of the other cases.*

THE HOMESTEAD BILL.

The Homestead Bill, as it is called, has been advocated by its friends upon the principle that the United States had the power, under the express clause of the Constitution, to dispose of the public lands for any purpose which would promote the interests of the United States, and that those interests would be more advanced by granting a quarter section of land to every citizen who would build a house upon it and reside there with his family, and cultivate a crop each year for five years, than by keeping them out of market waiting for a purchaser, and then permitting them to go into the hands of speculators in vast quantities, to be held at prices ranging from $10 to $20 per acre, as is now the case with many millions of acres in the new States. *My own idea* is that the true policy would.be to stop the public sales altogether, and to grant the lands or sell them at advanced prices to actual settlers only, and that in quantities not exceeding one quarter section. Experience has proven that wherever the lands were surveyed and brought into market before the country was settled, the majority of the lands, comprising the timber, water privileges, and most valuable portions, have been purchased by capitalists and speculators in the old States, who have immediately raised the price to $5 and $10 per acre, and waited until the few scattered settlers, by their improvements, should create demand and increase the value; while in those portions of the country where the Government failed to complete the surveys, and bring the lands into market, for several years after the Indian title was extinguished, emigrants poured into the country in the mean time, and each settler occupied one quarter section for the use of his own family, and the country became more densely populated before the lands were offered in market than those other portions of the country were in twenty years after the lands were sold. This fact accounts for the denser population in the southern counties of Minnesota, and in the northern counties of Illinois, as also for the sparse settlements in a large portion of Iowa.

The public lands stand on a different footing from money raised by taxation, and the discretion of Congress *only* controls the mode and manner of their disposition; but Congress is bound by a moral obligation to exercise the power for the good of the Union.

Reverting to the system of survey, I here call your attention to the fact that all persons must purchase "*legal subdivisions.*" No one can buy by the single acre, unless that happens to be a legal subdivision—that is, a *fractional* quarter section containing only that amount.

Figure 6 is designed to show what is done with the fractions. It represents part of a township lying on the Illinois River. It will be observed that section 16 is complete, and that sections 14, A B C, 15, C B D G H, 22, H G K, and 21, G F M N K, are fractional and incomplete.

A B C not being a fraction *within* any section, constitutes a section by itself, and would do so if it only contained a single acre, and would be described as *fractional section* 14, and so on. In the same figure we have a similar fraction, N O P, which does lie within a section, and *if* small in area, as we suppose in the present case, would be added to the N E fractional quarter, K G S P, and the whole would be described as the east fractional half of section 21, and so in any similar case.

THE PUBLIC LAND SYSTEM. 177

H G K in the figure is a fractional section.

If the fraction N O P were large enough to be surveyed, it would then be the S. E. fractional quarter of section 21.

If, in the case of B R H, the smaller portion were

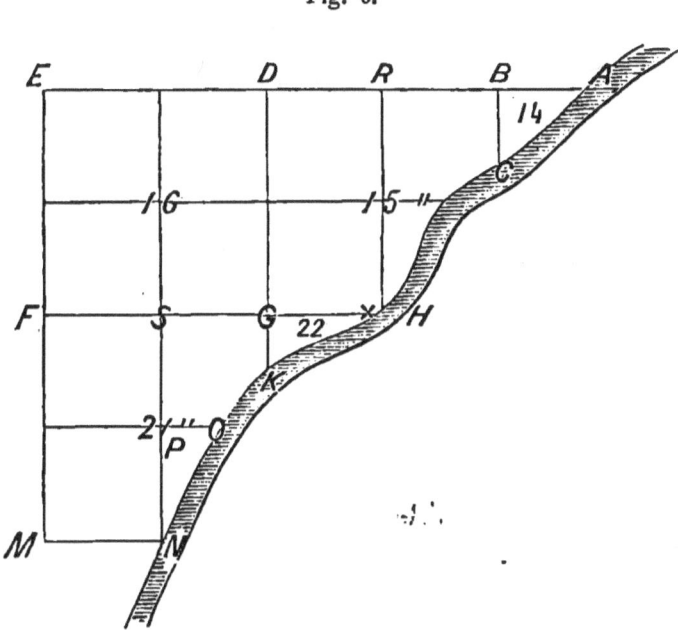

Fig. 6.

added to the greater, it would be indicated by dots (ıı) on its line, as in the figure, and it would be the east fractional half of section 15; so also the dots in G S P N O would indicate this addition of the smaller part, N O P. These marks are sometimes fraudulently erased, or accidentally omitted by the surveyor, and great speculations are sometimes made in these fractions. A case occurred some years ago where a man applied to enter five or ten acres in Cincinnati, which were built upon, and were immensely valuable, and the commissioner refused, on the ground that not knowing whether the dots had been there or not he would suppose them to be there, and Congress subsequently passed a law confirming the title of the other proprietors.

So also there was a case in Chicago involving the question whether these dots were on the line C D in figure 7 or not.

If the dots (ıı) were on the line C D, then C E F D was included in the fractional quarter section, section 10, I believe; so that it was included in the entry and purchase made by a man named Kinzie in 1815 or 1820. About 1835 Murray McConnell, being familiar with land speculations, came to Chicago, and, on looking over the map, concluded that C E F D was not so included, and he entered it. The people raised a mob and compelled him to give up his duplicate, and the land office rescinded the entry, and Congress subsequently passed a law confirming the Kinzie title. The lots had been subdivided by him, running down to the river as in the figure. A suit has now arisen between other parties involving title, and McConnell steps forward and claims it on the ground that he had entered it, and of being compelled by force to give it up, that the

Fig. 7.

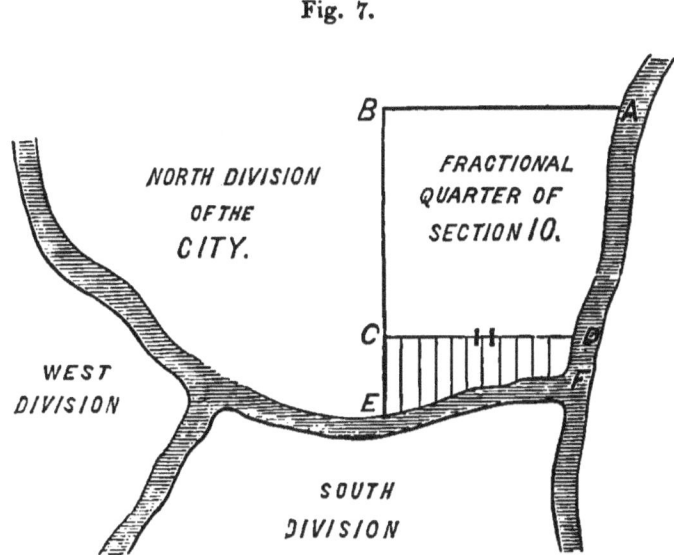

land office could not rescind the purchase, and that the subsequent act of Congress divesting title was unconstitutional, and therefore that the land is his. This case involves the question of the dots, and illustrates to you the speculations in fractions.

The Illinois Central Railroad case involves this principle again, arising out of the same tract of land. (See figure 8.)

Fig. 8.

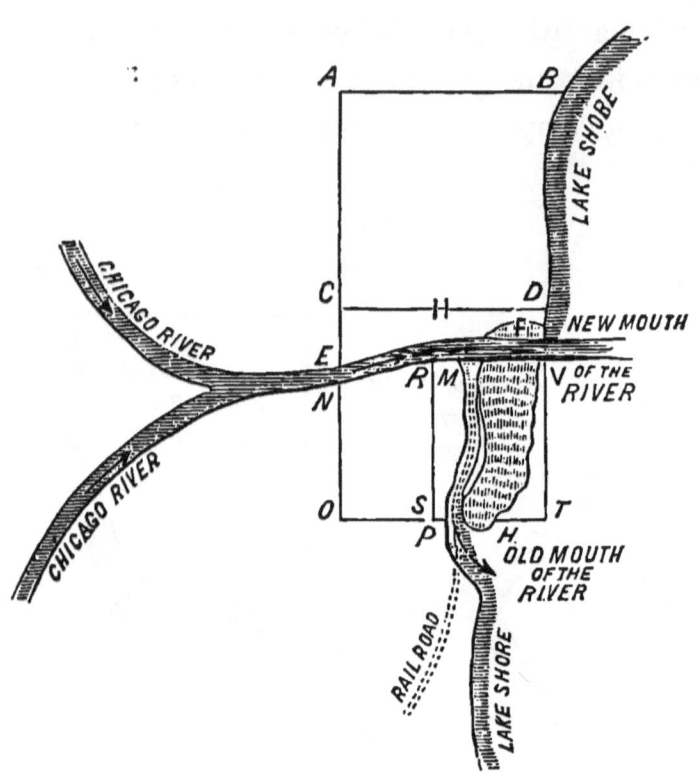

In the first place, were these dots or cross lines on the line C D, as in the last case?

The Chicago River formerly took a bend, leaving the sand-bar F H. An appropriation being made for the improvement of the Chicago River and harbor, the engineer cut right through this bar as indicated above, and it was subsequently washed away. M N O P was a military reservation. The

Illinois Central Railroad brought their road into the city, in front of Michigan Avenue, on the lake, as indicated by the dotted lines, and bought of the War Department the small tract M R S P, so as to secure the water right, and then built out, by filling in, the square R S T V, on which they located their depots, and which comprises several acres, and is worth two millions of dollars.

A Mr. Bates bought the portion D C E F, which would include the sand-bar. I advised the railroad at the time of this fact, but they paid no attention to it. The sand-bar would be included in Mr. Bates' purchase. McConnell interposes his claim as already explained, and in all probability the railroad will have to pay either the one or the other.

I have stated that a man buys legal subdivision, but it is to be added that they are subdivisions *according to the maps and surveys of the United States*, which, though often inaccurate, are yet taken *to be true*, and no proof is admitted to the contrary. So that a man must buy according to their surveys, and consequently pays for whatever the maps show, and gets whatever there actually is, whether more or less than the maps indicate. The following figure will serve to show you the inaccuracies in the surveys:

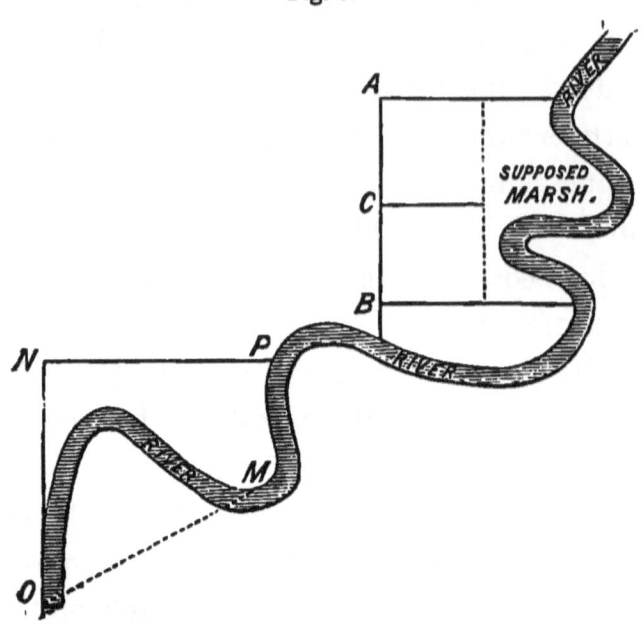

Suppose, first, a winding river, as they often are, and navigable.

The surveyor fixes upon *A*, as a point from which to measure his actional line A B, one mile in length, divides at C, and makes his survey as far toward the river as the dotted line, excluding the other as marsh land, and not worth any thing, and calling it fifty acres. A man buys this marsh land, and there is in reality one hundred acres. He pays for fifty and gets a hundred. Again, the river takes a bend, and the surveyor imagines a line M O, as if it took that direction, and calls M O N P one hundred and fifty acres, and there are but one hundred. Generally speaking, there is more land in these fractions than the maps show.

A preëmption right not entered and paid up is not transferable, or, in other words, all transfers of preëmption rights made before the patent issues are void. Good, of course, afterwards.

BOUNTY LANDS GIVEN TO SOLDIERS AND SPECULATIONS THEREIN.

After the close of the Mexican war, Congress passed a law granting one hundred and sixty acres of land to each volunteer for his military services, in addition to his pay, in the same manner as Congress had previously done for the soldiers in the war of 1812 with Great Britain. Since the Mexican war Congress had also made grants of bounty lands to all soldiers, whether in the war of 1812 or the Mexican war, or any of the Indian wars, of one hundred and sixty acres each, to all who had served a certain length of time, three months, as I recollect, or of eighty acres for a less period, which, I think, extended to at least fourteen days. A paper called a *land warrant* was issued to each soldier, specifying the particular service for which it was issued, the act of Congress authorizing it, and the amount of land to which he was entitled, which warrant he was at liberty to locate upon any of the surveyed lands of the United States which had been offered at public sale, and still remained unsold. By a subsequent act of Congress these land warrants were made assignable by endorsements upon the back, according to the form prescribed by the department. The warrants thus became a subject of speculation, the same as State bonds or any other securities, and were located by the holder in his own name, as the assignee of the soldier, and when presented at the land office were received in payment for the amount of lands specified in the warrant, in lieu of money, and the land officers were required in their reports to specify each tract of land thus paid for by warrant, in contradistinction to the lands sold for cash. These grants of land proved of no service to the poor men who were intended to be benefited. The land warrants were bought up for a song by land agents and speculators.

SALT SPRINGS.

When Ohio, Indiana, and Illinois were Territories, there were several salt springs in different portions of them, which were deemed valuable for the manufacture of salt, and which for that reason were reserved from public sale by the United States, and were leased to persons who wished to work them. When these States were admitted into the Union, the Government having found the management of the salt springs inconvenient, and costing more than the rents obtained for them, ceded them to the States in which they were situated. Since that time the grant of the salt springs in each new State has been made for no other or better reason than that there were precedents on the statute-book, and that each State claimed them, although the springs have ceased to be of any considerable value, and have nearly all been long since abandoned for salt works. In the grant to each State the number is limited to twelve, because, wherever there was brackish water, the State might undertake to consider it a salt spring, and on this pretext claim many entire sections of land.

BAD RESULTS OF LAND GRANTS.

One of the principal bad results has been, that they have produced great corruption in Congress in procuring the grants. It having been supposed that the Illinois Central Railroad would make immense profits in consequence of the great value of the lands granted, combinations were formed in other States where the public lands were situated, to procure charters from those States for the construction of railroads on certain specified lines, and containing clauses transferring to the companies all lands granted or to be granted by Congress in aid of the construction of the said roads. The corporators in these companies immediately acquired large pecuniary interest in procuring large grants from Congress, which would enure to themselves the moment they were granted, and, in order to procure these grants, would make combinations in Congress, by which they would convey in advance large tracts of land to the friends of the members of Congress as a compensation for their influence in procuring the grants.

HISTORY OF THE ILLINOIS CENTRAL RAILROAD BILL.

THE Illinois bill was the pioneer bill, and went through without a dollar, pure, uncorrupt, and is the only one which has worked well.

As early as 1835 the Illinois Legislature granted to D. B. Holbrooke a charter for the Illinois Central Railroad, and also for the construction of a city at the mouth of the Ohio River, called Cairo, and various other charters for enterprises connected with his proposed improvements at Cairo. Before Mr. Holbrooke had taken any steps to construct the road, the Illinois Legislature, at the session of 1836 and 1837, commenced a system of internal improvements at the expense and under the control of the State, which system embraced the construction of the Illinois Central Railroad among other works, and they repealed the charter granted to Mr. Holbrooke for that road. After spending a large amount of money on these various works, including over a million of dollars upon the Illinois Central road, the credit of the State failed during the pecuniary revulsion in 1837, 1838, 1839, and 1840, and the works were all abandoned. Mr. Holbrooke again applied to the State for a charter to construct the road, which was granted to him and to his associates, together with all the work that had been already done, on condition that he would proceed and construct the road. Mr. Holbrooke, through his friend and partner Judge Breese, Senator from Illinois, applied to Congress for a preëmption right to enter all the lands at any period within ten years, on each side of the line of said road, at one dollar and a quarter per acre, and Senator Breese reported a bill to that effect from the Committee on Public Lands of the Senate, and urged its passage. His colleague, Mr. Douglas, denounced the proposition as one of extravagant speculation, injurious to the interest of the State, inasmuch as its effect would be to withhold eight or ten million acres of land from settlement and cultivation for the period of ten years, until they should become valuable in consequence of the improvements made by the settlers upon the adjacent lands, without imposing any obligation on the company to make the road, or to pay for any of the lands, except those which they should in the mean time sell at advanced prices—the bill, in fact, creating a vast monopoly of the public lands. Mr. Douglas then introduced into the Senate a counter-proposition, which was to make the grant to the State of Illinois, of alternate sections. For details see the bill itself. Mr. Holbrooke and his agents used their influence to defeat this bill, because the grant was made to the State, instead of to the company. Mr. Douglas succeeded in passing it through the Senate, with almost a certain prospect of its passage in the House. When it was supposed that the grant was certain to become a law, Mr. Holbrooke and his agents went directly to Illinois, when the Legislature was in session, but at a time when no person in Illinois supposed that the bill would pass Congress, and procured the passage of a law making several important amendments to his charter. After the Legislature adjourned, and after the land grant had been defeated in Congress, *fortunately*, but unexpectedly, by two votes, Mr. Douglas returned home, and upon examining the manuscript acts of the Legislature before they were printed, discovered that a clause had been *surreptitiously* inserted into the amendments of Mr. Holbrooke's charter, conveying to his company all the lands granted or which should be granted to the State of Illinois, to aid in the construction of railroads in that State! This act purported to have passed the Illinois Legislature on the very day on which the final vote was taken in Congress upon the grant of lands. Upon inquiry of the Governor, Secretary of State, and members of the Legislature, they all denied any knowledge of this particular clause in the act, and no one could account for its being in the act, nor did any one know at what time it was inserted, or by whom. By an examination of the journals it appeared that the Legislature had at the same time passed resolutions instructing their Senators and requesting their Representatives in Congress to vote for the grant of land, although it had already passed the Senate, and all the Representatives were supporting it in the House. Mr. Douglas repaired immediately to Chicago, and made a public speech, in which he exposed this act of the Illinois Legislature in giving away the lands which Congress proposed to grant to the State, and denounced it as an act of fraud and corruption, and pledged himself to defeat any grant of land in Congress which should come to Mr. Holbrooke or his associates, or to anybody except the State of Illinois. It was never ascertained how the amendment was introduced; probably some enrolling clerk was bribed. When Congress assembled at the next session, Mr. Holbrooke made his appearance, and urged Mr. Douglas to renew his bill for the grant of land. Mr. Douglas showed him a bill which he was about to introduce, commencing the road at a *different point* on the Ohio River, and running it to Chicago on a *different line* from the Illinois Central, and making it a condition of the grant that it should not enure to any railroad company *then in existence*.

Mr. Holbrooke begged Mr. Douglas to save Cairo, where he had lodged his entire fortune. Mr. Douglas consented, provided he would release his charter for the road, and his charters for the various improvements at Cairo. Holbrooke went to New York, and as president of the company executed the release, and returned with it to Washington. Mr. Douglas then told him he thought he was a swindler, and had resolved to cheat somebody, but was not wise enough to cheat him, and that he ought to know, and did know, that neither the president nor the directors alone could make a valid release; that he must first summon a meeting of the stockholders, have them instruct the directors, and the directors instruct the president. He thereupon returned to New York, and brought back a satisfactory release, setting forth the meeting of the stockholders and of the directors. I had furnished him with an outline of a proper release. I don't know whether the stockholders ever did actually meet, but there was the seal, the signature, and the proceedings set forth, and that was enough. I immediately sent the release to the Secretary of State of Illinois, to be filed and recorded, and requested him to telegraph me upon its reception. I waited until I received the telegraphic despatch, and then called up the bill and passed it through the Senate. I had previously told Holbrooke that if he did not leave the city I would denounce him in *open* Senate, as I did to the Senate, and that I would not allow even a suspicion that so great a scoundrel as he, was in any way connected with the measure. The bill passed the House by three majority, and I was confined to my room in great pain by an abscess in my thigh, rendering a surgical operation necessary, when Mr. Holbrooke returned and walked into my room. I allowed his presence, it being no longer necessary to quarrel with him. We had some conversation, when he offered, if I would surrender the release, to deed to me one-half of the lands granted, over two and a half millions, and worth twenty millions. I jumped for my crutches, he ran from the room, and I gave him a parting blow on the head. He did not know that I had sent the release home to Illinois, to the Secretary of State.

The bill, when first introduced, had been opposed by the Senators from Mississippi, Davis and Foote, on the ground of its unconstitutionality, and also by the Senators from Alabama, King and Clemens, and by the members of the House from those States. Immediately after its first defeat, I went to my children's plantation in Mississippi, and from there to Mobile, intending to see the president of the Mobile Railroad, then building, but which had been stopped, and failed for want of means. I inquired the way to his office, found it and himself, and fortunately all the directors, who had just had a meeting, and knew what to do. I proposed to him to procure a grant of lands, by making it part of my Illinois Central Railroad Bill, which they assented to. I then told them that their Senators and Representatives must vote for the bill. They said they would. "No!" I replied, "they have already voted against it. It is necessary to instruct them by the Legislatures of your States." One of the directors, Foote, was related to Senator Foote, of Mississippi, and said he would have this done, and that Foote should never be reëlected to the Senate unless he did vote as was required. The others all thought they had sufficient influence to secure instructions from the Legislatures of Alabama and Mississippi. I told them it was necessary to keep quiet, and secret, as to my connection in the matter. They promised this, and we all returned to Montgomery, Alabama. They begged me to stop with them, but I went straight on to Washington, being afraid to be seen in those parts. After I arrived in Washington, the instructions came from Alabama, and King came, and cursed the Legislature. Davis did not know what in the world was the matter, and refused to believe it. Soon after came instructions, by telegraphic report, from Mississippi; Davis swore, and a few days after came his letters and written instructions. Then they wanted me to assist them. I told them, by way of brag, and to conceal my connection with their instructions, that they had refused to support my bill, and that I could carry it without them; but I finally yielded, and consented to King's proposition (I allowed it to come from him), to amend my bill, so as to connect the Mobile road—thus making a connection between the latter and the Gulf of Mexico. Some time afterwards I prepared an amendment—Mr. Rockwell, of Connecticut, a good lawyer, assisting me—and gave them notice that I was going to call up the bill in the Senate. When I did so, I found that Foote, Davis, King, and others were absent from the Senate room, and I sent a boy to their committee rooms to summon them. They came in haste, King saying that he had not prepared an amendment, and that he did not know what was required, and asking me to draw one for him. I told him I had anticipated this, and showed him the amendment which I had prepared. I then made my motion in the Senate, and Mr. King then rose, and with great dignity asked the Senator from Illinois to accept an amendment which he had to offer. I did so. They all voted for the bill, and it passed the Senate, and went to the House.

All this occurred during the excited times of slavery discussion and agitation in 1850.

When the bill stood at the head of the calendar, Harris, of Illinois, moved to proceed to clear the Speaker's table, and the motion was carried. We had counted up, and had fifteen majority for the bill pledged to support it. We had gained votes by lending our support to many local measures. The House proceeded to clear the Speaker's table, and the Clerk announced " A bill granting lands to the State of Illinois," et cetera. Then you could see the opposition start up. A motion was immediately made by the opposition, which brought on a vote, and we found ourselves in a minority of one. I was standing in the lobby, paying eager attention, and would have given the world to be at Harris's side, but was too far off to get there in time; and it was all in an instant, and the next moment a motion would have been made, which would have brought on a decided vote, and have defeated the bill. Harris, quick as thought, pale and white as a sheet, jumped to his feet, and moved that the House go into committee of the whole on the slavery question. There were fifty members ready with speeches on this subject, and the motion was carried. Harris came to me in the lobby, and asked me if he had made the right motion. I said, " Yes," and asked him if he knew what was the effect of his motion. He replied it placed the bill at the foot of the calendar. I asked him how long it would be before it came up again. He said, " it would not come up this session; it was impossible, there were ninety-seven bills ahead of it." Why not then have suffered defeat? It was better that we did not. We then racked our brains, or I did, for many nights, to find a way to get at the bill, and at last it occurred to me that the same course pursued with the other bills would place them, each in its turn, at the foot of the calendar, and thus bring the Illinois bill at the head. But how to do this was the question. The motions to clear the Speaker's table, and to go into " committee of the whole" on the slavery question, would each have to be made *ninety-seven times*, and while the first motion might be made by some of our friends, or the friends of the other bills, it would not do for us, or any one known to be a warm friend or connected with us, to make the second motion, as it would defeat the other bills, and alienate from us the support of their friends. I thought a long while, and finally fixed on Mr. —— of ——, who, though bitterly opposed to me, we having often had warm and excited passages of arms on political questions, I yet knew to be my warm admirer and personal friend. Living up in ——, he supported the bill, but did not care much one way or the other whether it passed or not; voted for it, but was lukewarm. I called him aside one day, stated my case, and asked him if he would place me under obligations to him by making the second motion, as often as was necessary. He said yes, provided that Mr. ——, of ——, whom he hated, should have no credit in the event of the success of the measure. I replied that he would have none. Harris, then in the House, sometimes twice on the same day, on others once, either made himself, or caused the friends of the other bills to make the first motion, when Mr. —— would immediately make the second. All praised us; said we were acting nobly in supporting them. We replied, "Yes, having defeated our bill, we thought we would be generous, and assist you." All cursed Mr. ——. Some asked me if I had not influence enough to prevent his motion. I replied, he was an ardent antagonist, and that I had nothing to do with him, to the truth of which they assented. Finally, by this means, the Illinois bill got to the head of the docket. Harris, that morning, made the first motion. We had counted noses, and found, as we thought, twenty-eight majority, all pledged. The Clerk announced "a bill granting lands to the State of Illinois," and so on, reading by its title. The opposition again started, were taken completely by surprise, said there must be some mistake, that the bill had gone to the foot of the calendar. It was explained, and the Speaker declared it all right. A motion was immediately made by the opposition to go into committee of the whole; it was negatived by *one* majority, and we passed the bill by *three* majority.

If any man ever passed a bill, I did that one. I did the whole work, and was devoted to it for two entire years. The people in Illinois are beginning to forget it. It is sometimes said, " Douglas never made a speech upon it." The Illinois Central Railroad Company hold their lands now by virtue of the release from Holbrooke, which I procured.

INDIANS AND INDIAN INTERCOURSE LAWS.

The Government of the United States recognizes the possessory right of the Indian tribes to the country occupied by them, and protects the Indians in the enjoyment of such rights against molestation or invasion by anybody. While it recognizes this possessory right in the Indians, of which they cannot be deprived without their consent, it denies the irright to dispose of their lands, or to hold intercourse with anybody except the United States or their duly appointed agents. The mode adopted for extinguishing the Indian title is by treaty between the United States and the several tribes, which treaties, like all other treaties, are to be ratified by the Senate. In order to protect the Indians in their right to occupy their lands, Congress has enacted a system of laws which are usually known as the "Indian Intercourse Laws." These laws make it a criminal offence for any person to invade or enter the Indian Territories without permission of the Government, or to trade with the Indians in any respect whatever, and also make it a criminal offence for the Government agents or anybody else to sell ardent spirits to the Indians. They provide for the appointment of Indian agents by the President and Senate, to reside among the various tribes, and to see that the Indians are not molested by white people, and that the intercourse laws are not violated either by the Indians or whites. They provide also for the appointment of licensed traders among the various tribes, who supply the Indians with blankets, clothing, provisions, and other articles adapted to their use, at certain fixed rates of profit above the wholesale cost, and prohibit all other persons from trading with the Indians. They provide also for the appointment of persons called "farmers," who reside among the Indians, and teach them the arts of agriculture, the use of the implements, and the mode of planting, cultivating, and preserving the crops. These traders, farmers, and licensed persons residing among the Indians, are all under the general superintendence of the Indian agents of the respective tribes, and these agents themselves act under the direction and instructions of the Superintendent of Indian Affairs for each territory or district for which a superintendent is appointed; and the superintendents act under the direct authority of, and are responsible to, the Commissioner of Indian Affairs, who resides in Washington, and is the head of the Bureau in the Department of the Interior known as the Indian Bureau.

THE RECIPROCITY TREATY.

The increase of population and business along the entire extent of our Northern frontier, and upon the great lakes, rendered a more intimate and liberal intercourse between the Canadas and the United States necessary to the interest and convenience of both countries, and also created a necessity for procuring, on the part of the United States, the right to use and navigate the Welland Canal, connecting Lakes Erie and Ontario, and by which the Falls of Niagara are avoided; and also for the navigation of the river St. Lawrence, and the use of the locks and short canals around the falls, and obstructions in said river.

The necessity for an arrangement to cover these points was deeply felt by the Canadians as well as by the Americans interested in the trade of the great lakes. As an illustration of the inconveniences arising out of the former restrictive policy, it will be borne in mind that the transportation from Chicago and all other points west to the eastward, consisted chiefly in wheat, corn, beef, pork, and other heavy and bulky articles; whereas the freights up the lakes, westward, consisted in drygoods, manufactured articles, and ordinary merchandise, so that *one* vessel freighted with these articles could carry up the lakes goods of sufficient value to pay for the freight of *ten* vessels down the lakes, and consequently a large portion of the vessels which carried full cargoes down the lakes were under the necessity of returning with very slight or no cargoes. It soon became the habit of vessels to touch upon the Canadian shore, and to take in building-stone, firewood, and lumber, for the purposes of ballast. But when they arrived in Chicago with their cargoes, the duty was frequently greater than the value of the cargo, and the consequence was that hundreds of vessels were known to throw their entire cargo overboard into the lake, rather than pay the duty, and this at a time when the articles were in demand at Chicago and at all other points on the lakes. These inconveniences were felt also in the shipments of wheat and other American products from the upper lakes to Oswego, and other points below on their way to New York, not only in consequence of the high duties on the Welland Canal, but from the fact that they had to pay duties in Canada for the importation of those articles from the United States, *when they were only in transitu;* while the Canadians, who found it to their interest during a great portion of the year, when the St. Lawrence was closed by ice, to send their wheat and other products to New York by the railroads and canals, were prevented from doing so by the duties which they were compelled to pay by the United States, in consequence of entering our territory.

These considerations suggested the propriety of an arrangement between the two countries by which certain articles of growth and manufacture in each might enter the other free of duty, and permitting the United States to use the canals and the St. Lawrence River for purposes of navigation on an equal footing with the British subjects, and without paying any other or higher duties. Failing to procure any such arrangement by treaty, General Dix, of New York, Mr. Douglas, and others, proposed bills in the Senate, making the propositions in the form of *reciprocal legislation*, for the accomplishment of their object. Pending these measures, however, a treaty was made between the United States and Great Britain, which is known as the Reciprocity Treaty, by which these objects were accomplished. This was in 1850 or 1851.

THE MONROE DOCTRINE.

WHAT is known as the "Monroe Doctrine" had its origin and name in a recommendation of President Monroe, in one of his messages to Congress, at a time when Spain was making arrangements to reconquer and subdue her various colonies in America which had revolted, and established their independence in 1819–'20, and '21. It was apprehended by the American Government that the despotic powers of Europe, after the overthrow of Napoleon and the reëstablishment of the despotic sway in Europe, would lend their aid to conquer and subject these Spanish colonies, which had then become independent States; and that while a portion of them would, in this event, be restored to Spain, the others might be divided among the various powers of Europe. In view of this probable result, President Monroe declared, in his message to Congress, with a view of its being taken as notice to all Europe, that no portion of the American continent was hereafter to be deemed open to European colonization, and that the United States would consider any such attempt as imposing upon them the obligation to take such steps as were necessary to prevent it. This declaration assumed the name of the Monroe Doctrine; and it has frequently been appealed to by American statesmen as a rule *to be inflexibly adhered to,* whenever any European power has threatened or attempted to extend its dominions upon the American continent—North, South, or Central America. This doctrine did not contemplate any interference on the part of the United States with the existing rights or colonial possessions of any European power, *but was a protest against the extension of their power and policy in the future.*

CENTRAL AMERICA.

THE CLAYTON AND BULWER TREATY.

The oldest possession which Great Britain claims in Central America is that which is known as the "Balize Settlement," dividing Nicaragua and Honduras on the one side from the Mexican State of Yucatan on the other. More than a century ago some British merchants sent out ships, and cut and loaded them with logwood at the Balize, which at that time belonged to Spain. In making a treaty of peace between Spain and England, a clause was inserted continuing the permission to cut logwood, without conveying any right of soil or dominion to England. Under the permission to cut logwood, England founded a settlement at the Balize, with no fixed or definite boundaries; and she has enlarged and extended it from time to time, and organized it into a colony, without paying any attention to the territorial rights or boundaries of the adjoining States.

About the same time England pretended to have made a treaty with a small tribe of Indians called the Mosquitos, upon the coast of Central America, and to have guaranteed to the Indians the protection of the British Government. Some years ago, perhaps twenty, the British Government sent an agent to the Mosquito coast, and found an Indian boy—part Indian and part mulatto—who was said to have been the son of a Mosquito Indian chief, and took him over to Jamaica and had him crowned as the king of the Mosquitos, took him back again to his own country, and put him in nominal possession of his alleged inheritance, but, in fact, under the direction and control of a British consul on that coast. This Mosquito country was within the chartered limits of the State of Nicaragua, and consequently the Indian tribes, the Mosquitos included, were subjects of the State of Nicaragua, and incapable of establishing a government independent of that State.

This was the condition of affairs in Central America when the war between the United States and Mexico was brought to a close. It was understood, and in fact not denied, that Great Britain used her entire powers of diplomacy to encourage Mexico, and to defeat any treaty of peace by which the United States would acquire any Mexican territory. On the day that it became known at Vera Cruz that a treaty of peace had been signed, by which California and New Mexico were transferred to the United States, the British fleet set sail from Vera Cruz and proceeded directly to the mouth of the San Juan River, in Central America, and took possession of the town of San Juan at the mouth of the river, changed its name to Greytown, and established British authority there, in the name of the Mosquito king, to be exercised by the British consul, and, in fact, converted into a British dependency. The United States protested against this act, as being an aggression upon the territorial rights of Nicaragua, and as being prompted by hostile motives toward the United States, it having for its object to close up the only channel through which the United States could establish and maintain communication between the Atlantic States and our newly acquired possessions on the Pacific.

The controversy growing out of this seizure of that transit route lead to the Clayton and Bulwer treaty. It is proper, however, to remark, that during the last years of Mr. Polk's administration, he had appointed Judge Hise, of Kentucky, minister to the Central American States, and that Judge Hise had negotiated a treaty on the part of the United States, with the State of Nicaragua, by which the United States were invested with the exclusive right of constructing a ship canal between the Atlantic and Pacific Oceans, through the San Juan River and Lake Nicaragua, together with the right of establishing towns and free ports at each end of the canal, and of fortifying the same and placing the whole line of the canal and its banks, from ocean to ocean, under the *exclusive protection* of the United States. This Hise treaty was signed in Central America while Mr. Polk was President, but did not reach the United States until after the inauguration of General Taylor, and the appointment of Mr. Clayton as Secretary of State. Mr. Clayton refused to accept this treaty, and sent an agent to Central America to have it cancelled, and a new treaty made by which the said canal should be placed under the *joint protection* of Great Britain and the United States. Mr. Clayton then negotiated with Sir Henry Bulwer the Clayton treaty, by which his scheme of a joint protection to the transit route was recognized, and a provision inserted, by which Great Britain and the United

States pledged their faith, each to the other, that neither of them would ever colonize, annex, fortify, or exercise exclusive dominion over any portion of Central America. After the terms of this treaty were agreed to by Clayton and Bulwer, Mr. Clayton refused to sign it until he could procure from two-thirds of the Senators a private pledge that they would ratify it, which being done, he signed the treaty, and sent it to the Senate for ratification. Mr. Douglas was the only man in the Senate who made any active opposition to the ratification of the treaty. He opposed it upon the ground that he wanted no partnerships with Great Britain in respect to the transit route; that such a partnership would be productive of constant misunderstanding and disputes, instead of being a bond of peace; and he urged that the Senate reject the treaty, and call upon the Executive to send to the Senate the Hise treaty, that it might be ratified, with such amendments as the Senate might see fit to make, in order that we should have the exclusive control over the transit route, and might open it to the world on such terms as were compatible with American interests. Mr. Douglas especially opposed the treaty, upon the ground that he would never enter into any compact with Great Britain or any other European power in respect to the American continent, by which the faith of the nation should be pledged, for all time to come, never to annex or colonize such portions of the continent as our interest and safety would inevitably compel us to annex at some future day. He did not desire to annex the country then, but insisted that the time would come when we would be compelled to exercise jurisdiction over that transit route. All objection, however, to the treaty proved useless, as nearly the whole Senate had been committed to it privately, in advance, and when the vote was taken there were but eight votes recorded in the negative in the whole Senate.

The main argument urged in favor of the ratification of the treaty, was that it drove Great Britain out of Central America, by abolishing the British protectorate over the Mosquito coast. To this Mr. Douglas replied, that while Great Britain had no right to any protectorate over that coast, such pretended right *was not abolished* by the treaty, but on the contrary, equivocal language was used in it, which, when ratified, Great Britain would claim recognized the existence of such protectorate, and gave her the right to maintain it in the future.

The treaty had been no sooner ratified, than Great Britain *did claim* that her protectorate was still in existence, recognized and acknowledged by the United States, and she has from that day to this persisted in this claim to a protectorate.

All this occured in secret session in 1850, and within the next three years I tried often to get the Senate to remove the *injunction of secrecy*, so that I might publish my views. In 1853, three years afterwards, the English extended their influence, and took possession of Ruatan. Cass, in the Senate, began to get frightened. All that I had predicted had come to pass. Cass made a speech denouncing Clayton and the treaty. This was occurring about the time when Clayton retired from the office of Secretary of State. Soulé entered into the discussion, and in the course of their speeches, both he and Cass, forgetting that the injunction of secrecy had not been removed, quoted what had occurred during the secret session of 1850, or thereabouts. Nobody interrupted them, and I thought now is the time to get my speech and my views before the public, so I went to a Senator and said to him, "Look here, Soulé and Cass are quoting what occurred in secret session; suppose you move the Senate to go into secret session, and have the injunction removed, so that they can do so." The Senator started up, mischievously; Soulé apologized, said he was not aware that the injunction had not been removed; the Senate went into secret session, and the injunction was removed.

Clayton retired from the office of Secretary of State, went back to Delaware, and said Cass had been abusing and slandering him, and that it was necessary for him to reply, in order to vindicate himself, promising to annihilate Cass. He was re-elected to the Senate, and could have annihilated Cass, for the latter had taken the wrong ground, and Clayton was very powerful in debate.

Cass vanished, said his wife was sick, and that he had to go home to Detroit. Clayton came on ready with a speech, which would have just fitted Cass, and asked where he was. He was told Cass's wife was sick, and that he had gone home, and then turning to me, said, " No matter, what he had to say could equally be addressed to me as Cass's follower." When Clayton got through, I made my speech, which used him up. I stated all that I had previously said in the secret session, when the treaty was ratified, and a good deal more. The speech made a great impression upon the country, and gained me great fame and reputation, *and the treaty has been odious ever since.*

THE PACIFIC RAILROAD.

The first idea of a railroad to the Pacific originated more than twenty years ago, and the first demonstration that I am aware of in favor of the project was in a public meeting at Dubuque, Iowa, about 1838. A man by the name of Eli Whitney some fifteen years ago petitioned Congress to make a grant of one hundred millions of acres of land to him, to enable him to construct a railroad to the Pacific, and offered, as security for the faithful application of the lands to that object, *the pledge of his honor*, he being a broken-down merchant at the time, and having no means of support, and he now keeps a dairy farm near this city. His application was renewed for several sessions, and was backed by a large number of speculators in and out of Congress, but it received very little favor.

The measure was more seriously entertained

after the acquisition of New Mexico and California, and the settlement of the northern boundary of Oregon, and the organization of the Oregon Territory. As early as 1845, Mr. Douglas proposed a grant of alternate sections of land to the States of Ohio, Indiana, Illinois, and Iowa, to aid in the construction of a railroad from Lake Erie, *via* Chicago and Rock Island, to the Missouri River, and prepared a bill to organize the Territory of Nebraska, extending from the Missouri River to the summit of the Rocky Mountains, and the Territory of Oregon, to extend from the same summit to the Pacific Ocean, and to reserve to each of said Territories the alternate sections of land for forty miles on each side of a line of railroad, from such point on the Missouri River as the road from Lake Erie should cross the same, and thence to the navigable waters of the Pacific, in the Territory of Oregon, or on the Bay of San Francisco, *in the event that California should be annexed in time.* Not that this annexation was then improbable, but this was inserted to attract public attention to the subject. With a view of calling public attention to the importance of this road, Mr. Douglas issued an address to the people of Illinois, in support of the measure, which was widely circulated throughout the country.

Since the admission of California into the Union in 1850, a project for a Pacific Railroad has been introduced into both Houses of Congress at each session, and has been favorably reported upon by a select committee in each House. The main provisions of these bills were, that Congress should make an appropriation of lands, varying in the different bills from fifteen to forty sections per mile, from the Missouri River to the Pacific Ocean, and then providing that the President of the United States should receive sealed proposals from contractors for the construction of the road; the contractors to construct the road at their own expense, and to own it as their property, when constructed; and that the United States would make a donation of the lands to be conveyed to the company so far and so fast as the road should be completed through the same; and that the United States would make a contract in advance for the transportation of the United States mails, army and navy supplies, and all other freights for the use of the Government at fair prices to be determined by the bids. These bids were to be received on the following points: *first*, within how short a time will the contractors complete the road? *second*, at what rate per annum will the contractors carry the mails and other Government freight, for a period of twenty years, from the completion of the road? When all the bids were received, it was made the duty of the President, in the presence of his Cabinet, and such other persons as chose to be present, to open the bids and assign the contract to those contractors whose bids should be most favorable to the interests of the United States, having in view the shortness of time within which they would construct the road, and the cheapness of transportation upon it. The last bill reported to the Senate also proposed that the United States should loan to the contractors their five per cent. bonds to the amount of twelve thousand five hundred dollars per mile, for each mile of the road, which was to be repaid to the United States in mail and other Government service upon the road.

During the Presidential canvass of 1856, the Democratic party pledged itself, by a resolution of the Cincinnati Convention, to support a Pacific Railroad; and the Republican party, by a resolution of their National Convention at Philadelphia, gave a similar pledge; and during the canvass, each of the Presidential candidates, Buchanan, Fremont, and Fillmore, wrote letters advocating the measure. But notwithstanding these pledges by all the parties and all the candidates, the friends of the measure have never been able to get a majority vote in its favor in either House of Congress. I doubt whether there has been a majority for the measure ; not a majority in fact, only a professing majority. They are divided on routes and plans.

Can a great work like this go in advance of the growth and settlement of the country ?

No, it will hardly be executed in advance of the growth and settlement of the country.

THE END.

D. APPLETON & CO.'S PUBLICATIONS.

A STANDARD BOOK OF REFERENCE.

THE
HOUSEHOLD BOOK OF POETRY.

Collected and Edited by CHARLES A. DANA.

Tenth Edition. Royal 8vo. 798 pp. Beautifully printed.

Half mor., gilt top, $; half calf, extra, $; mor. ant., $.

"The purpose of this book is to comprise within the bounds of a single volume whatever is truly beautiful and admirable among the minor poems of the English language. * * * Especial care has also been taken to give every poem entire and unmutilated, as well as in the most authentic form which could be procured."—*Extract from Preface.*

"This work is an immense improvement on all its predecessors. The editor, who is one of the most erudite of scholars, and a man of excellent taste, has arranged his selections under ten heads, namely: Poems of Nature, of Childhood, of Friendship, of Love, of Ambition, of Comedy, of Tragedy and Sorrow, of the Imagination, of Sentiment and Reflection, and of Religion. The entire number of poems given is about two thousand, taken from the writings of English and American poets, and including some of the finest versions of poems from ancient and modern languages. The selections appear to be admirably made, nor do we think that it would be possible for any one to improve upon this collection."—*Boston Traveller.*

"Within a similar compass, there is no collection of poetry in the language that equals this in variety, in richness of thought and expression, and of poetic imagery."—*Worcester Palladium.*

"This is a choice collection of the finest poems in the English language, and supplies in some measure the place of an extensive library. Mr. Dana has done a capital service in bringing within the reach of all the richest thoughts that grace our standard poetical literature."—*Chicago Press.*

" A work that has long been required, and, we are convinced from the selections made, and the admirable manner in which they are arranged, will commend itself at once to the public."—*Detroit Advertiser.*

" Never was a book more appropriately named. By the exercise of a sound and skilful judgment, and a thorough familiarity with the poetical productions of all nations, the compiler of this work has succeeded in combining, within the space of a single volume, nearly every poem of established worth and compatible length in the English language."—*Philadelphia Journal.*

" It gives us in an elegant and compact form such a body of verse as can be found in no other volume or series of volumes. It is by far the most complete collection that has ever been made of English lyrical poetry."—*Boston Transcript.*

" Among the similar works which have appeared we do not hesitate to give this the highest place."—*Providence Journal.*

" We are acquainted with no selections which, in point of completeness and good taste, excel the 'Household Book of Poetry.'"—*Northwestern Home Journal.*

" It is almost needless to say that it is a mine of poetic wealth."—*Boston Post.*

THE NEW
AMERICAN CYCLOPÆDIA.

D. APPLETON & CO.,
443 & 445 Broadway,

HAVE NOW READY THE

NEW AMERICAN CYCLOPÆDIA,
A POPULAR DICTIONARY OF GENERAL KNOWLEDGE.

EDITED BY

GEORGE RIPLEY and CHARLES A. DANA,

AIDED BY A

Numerous Select Corps of Writers in all Branches of Science, Art, and Literature,

IN 16 LARGE VOLUMES, 8vo,

750 double-column Pages in each Volume.

From the New York Times.

"It is a work written by Americans for Americans. It proffers them the knowledge they most require, selected and arranged by those who are competent to the task, because they themselves had experienced the want they now endeavor to supply. It is minute on points of general interest, and condensed in those of more partial application. Its information is the latest extant, and in advance of any other book of reference in the world. The best talent in the country has been engaged in its production."

PRICE OF THE WORK:

In Extra Cloth, per vol.,	$5 00
In Library Leather, per vol.,	6 00
In Half Turkey Morocco, black, per vol.,	6 50
In Half Russia, extra gilt, per vol.,	7 50
In Full Morocco, antique, gilt edges, per vol.,	9 00
In Full Russia,	9 00

The price of the work will, for the present, remain as above, but if there shall be any great advance in paper and material the price must be increased. To prevent disappointment, orders should be at once forwarded to the publishers or to the agents of the work in different parts of the country.

To those who have not already Subscribed for the Work.

Many persons have omitted to subscribe for the Work during its progress through the Press, owing to an unwillingness to subscribe for an incomplete work. They may now obtain complete sets in any of the above Styles.

D. APPLETON & CO., Publishers,
443 & 445 Broadway, N. Y.

www.ingramcontent.com/pod-product-compliance
Lightning Source LLC
Chambersburg PA
CBHW021840230426
43669CB00008B/1029